Praying
In Inclusive Language:

TWENTY-TWO
GATHERING PRAYERS

**For Church Council Meetings
and
Family and Community Gatherings**

Rev. Joseph J. Arackal

Published by:

Sheed & Ward

P.O. Box 419492

Kansas City, MO 64141-6492

To order call: 1-800-333-7373

CONTENTS

INTRODUCTION

GATHERING PRAYERS

"Praying In Inclusive Language: Twenty-Two Gathering Prayers," is the product of the author's conviction that inclusive language is essential in nourishing, strengthening and expressing Faith. He believes that inclusive language is a matter of justice and that the continued use of exclusive language is a serious injustice.

Language, especially in the context of religion, is a very powerful tool in the formation of cultural and social attitudes. While inclusive language can truly enhance, augment, sustain, inspire and express faith, exclusive language can have lasting negative results.

Study of scriptures, both the Old Testament and the New Testament, reveals that the original scripture texts were inclusive in nature, but their translations into some of the modern languages have resulted in much of the exclusive language present in modern scripture. Inclusive language is much wider in its scope than gender-free language but obviously includes it.

"Praying In Inclusive Language: Twenty-Two Gathering Prayers," is prepared in accord with the directives approved by the U.S. Bishops during their November 12-15, 1990 general meeting. The inclusive scripture translations used in the Gathering Prayers are the author's rendition from the original texts that "respect the doctrinal principles of revelation, inspiration and biblical interpretation as well as the formal rhetoric intended by the (original) author."

OUTLINE OF THE GATHERING PRAYERS

Introductory verse
(Optional Light Service)
Hymn
Psalmody
2 Psalms with their antiphons
Reading
Responsory
Canticle of Mary with antiphon
Intercessions
The Abba Prayer of Jesus
Concluding Prayer

DIVINE TITLES

The Divine Name YAHWEH is the personal proper name of God that was revealed to Moses (Exodus 3:14-15). Yahweh means "I AM WHO AM" and refers to God as the Absolute Being Who is the Source of all created beings.

YAHWEH (LORD),

YAHWEH SABAOTH (LORD of Hosts),

ADONAI (Lord or My Lord),

EL (God),

ELOHIM (God),

ELYON (Most High),

SHADDAI (Almighty),

EL SHADDAI (God Almighty) etc. are some of the titles used in the Old Testament in reference to God. (If you are uncomfortable in pronouncing the Sacred Divine Name Yahweh, you may substitute ADONAI or LORD in its place.)

Jesus used the Aramaic word ABBA to address God (Mark 14:36). The term 'Abba' (Mark 14:36), that appears in Jesus' prayer in Gethsemane, had passed into the Pauline Churches and was used ecstatically in prayer (Gal. 4:6; Rom. 8:15) by the early Christians. This indeclinable emphatic Aramaic term of address "Abba," though traditionally translated as "Father," may be considered as an untranslatable title of God, Who is the Source of all life and loves us both as a Mother and a Father.

The Doxology "Glory to Abba our God, to Christ the Word, and to the Holy Spirit etc." is an acclamation expressly attributing glory to the Triune God. It is an adaptation of the non-biblical doxology formula "Glory be to the Father, and to the Son, and to the Holy Spirit etc." introduced by the Syrian Church in the 4th century and eventually accepted by the universal Church.

GATHERING PRAYERS

INTRODUCTORY VERSE

Gathering Prayer begins with the Introductory Verse "O God, Come to my assistance" and "Glory to Abba" etc. This introduction is a call to prayer and a brief expression of praise and thanks. When celebrated in common all stand and make the sign of the cross as the leader of prayer says: "O God, come to my assistance" etc.

LIGHT SERVICE

After the Introductory Verse, the leader of prayer lights an oil lamp or a candle as may be convenient. During the lamp/candle lighting one of the prayers found on page 45 may be said or an appropriate hymn sung or silence kept. Incense may be used during the light service as a sign of the community's prayer rising to God: "May our prayer be set before You like incense."

HYMN

An appropriate hymn follows the Introductory Verse and the Light Service to set the tone of Hour of Prayer. Hymns chosen, as far as possible, must fit into the context of the gathering and the season of the year.

PSALMODY

Psalms are the heart of the Prayers of the Church and are chosen to correspond to the particular hour of the day. The recitation of the psalms is concluded with the "Glory to Abba" etc. giving these Old Testament prayers a quality of praise as well as adding a Christological and Trinitarian aspect.

During the recitation of the psalms all may sit. Two groups may alternate praying the stanzas of the psalms. The antiphon provided for each psalm or canticle serves as a theme statement of the psalm or canticle. It will also help us to turn the psalm into a personal prayer by highlighting a verse or phrase of the psalm. The antiphon is prayed by the entire group both in the beginning and at the end of the psalm or canticle. On occasion the antiphon may be used as a response after each verse of the psalm, in the manner of a responsorial psalm.

The psalmody for the "Gathering Prayers" consists of two psalms with their antiphons. Other psalms or canticles (page 46) may be used in the place of the psalms provided.

Silent Prayer

After the psalm is prayed and antiphon repeated, a brief moment of silence is observed. This moment of silent prayer helps one to see the psalm in a Christian light. Silence is observed in the beginning of a prayer as a means of recollection and at the conclusion of a reading, psalm or canticle to meditate briefly on what has been heard or recited.

READING

A short reading from scripture follows the Psalmody. Other scripture texts suitable for the season or occasion and for the time of the day may be chosen in the place of the selections provided. All are seated during the reading. After the reading a period of silence may be observed, followed by a brief homily or reflection.

RESPONSORY

After the Reading and the reflection, the short responsory or another responsorial song may be sung or recited.

GOSPEL CANTICLE

After the response to the Word of God, the Canticle of Mary is sung or recited with its antiphon. This canticle is an expression praise and thanksgiving for God's wonderful work of salvation finding fulfillment in Christ Jesus. During the singing of the Gospel Canticle incense may be used.

INTERCESSIONS

In the General Intercessions, we pray for the needs of the all the members of the human family. Prayers are offered for the Church, for civil authorities, for those oppressed by various needs, for all people, and especially for the special needs of the local community. There are two ways of praying the suggested intercessions:

a. after the brief introduction, one person may say the entire petition and everyone may repeat the response indicated by "R.";

b. or the first part of the petition is said by one person, and the second part, marked with a "—" is prayed by all.

On occasion, the leader of prayer may begin with a brief introduction and invite the community to express their individual intentions. The whole assembly gives expression to its supplication by a response prayed together after each intention. Other responses may replace those that are suggested.

THE ABBA PRAYER OF JESUS

At the conclusion of the intercessions, the leader of prayer leads the community in the singing or recitation of the Abba Prayer of Jesus (the Lord's Prayer) with a brief introduction.

CONCLUDING PRAYER

The concluding prayer attempts to express the theme of the celebration and the community's petition to Abba our God through Christ the Word and the Holy Spirit.

GATHERING PRAYERS 1:
Your Works Are Full of Majesty and Luster.

INTRODUCTORY VERSE

(All stand and make the sign of the cross as the leader of prayer says:)

    O God, come to my assistance.
    R. Yahweh, make haste to help me.

All: Glory to Abba our God, to Christ the Word, and to the
    Holy Spirit.
    As it was in the beginning,
    is now and will be for ever. Amen.

HYMN

(An appropriate hymn is sung.)

PSALMODY

(During the recitation of the psalms all may sit. Two groups may alternate praying the stanzas of the psalm. The antiphon is recited by the entire group.)

Psalm 111 A Hymn to Praise the Goodness of Yahweh

Antiphon 1

    I give You thanks, O Yahweh, with all my heart.

    I give You thanks, O Yahweh, with all my heart,
    in the company and assembly of the just.
    Great are Your works, O Yahweh,
    to be pondered by all who delight in them.

    Your works are full of majesty and luster
    and Your justice endures for ever.
    You have made a memorial of wonderful works;
    and You, Yahweh, are compassionate and merciful.

    You provide food for those who revere You;
    and You are ever mindful of Your covenant.
    You have shown Your people the power of Your works,
    in giving them the heritage of the nations.
    he works of Your hands are faithful and just,
    all Your precepts are trustworthy.
    They are established for ever and ever,
    to be performed with devotion and integrity.

    You have sent deliverance to Your people;
    You have commanded Your covenant for ever.
    Holy and awesome is Your Name!

    'The reverence of Yahweh is the root of wisdom;
    and wise are all those who practice it.'
    Your praise, Yahweh, endures for ever!

All: Glory to Abba our God, to Christ the Word,
    and to the Holy Spirit.
    As it was in the beginning,
    is now and will be for ever. Amen.

Antiphon 1

    I give You thanks, O Yahweh, with all my heart.

Silent Prayer

Psalm 119:1-8 God's Law, Our Source of Happiness: A Meditative Prayer.

Antiphon 2

    I will praise You with integrity of heart,
    as I learn Your just decrees, O God.

    Blessed are those whose way is perfect,
    who walk in the law of Yahweh!
    Blessed are those who keep Your instructions,
    who seek You with their whole heart.

    (Blessed are those) who do no wrong,
    and walk in Your ways!
    It was You Who commanded
    Your precepts to be diligently observed.

    O that my ways were faithful
    in observing Your statutes!
    Then I should not be ashamed,
    when I look to all Your commands.

    I will praise You with integrity of heart,
    as I learn Your just decrees.
    I will observe Your statutes;
    do not forsake me, O Eternal One!

All: Glory to Abba our God, to Christ the Word,
    and to the Holy Spirit.
    As it was in the beginning,
    is now and will be for ever. Amen.

Antiphon 2

    I will praise You with integrity of heart,
    as I learn Your just decrees, O God.

Silent Prayer

READING Romans 11:33-36

(All are seated during the reading.)

O the depth of wealth, wisdom and knowledge of God!
How unsearchable are God's judgments!
How inscrutable are God's ways!
Who has ever known the mind of Yahweh?
Who has ever been God's adviser?

Who has given a gift to God to receive a gift in return!
Source, Guide, and Goal of all things is God
and to Whom be glory for ever. Amen.

*(After the reading a period of silence may be observed
followed by a brief shared reflection.)*

RESPONSORY

Be still, and remember that I am God.
R. Supreme over all nations, supreme on the earth.

Holy and awesome is Your Name,
R. supreme on the earth.

Glory to Abba our God, to Christ the Word, and to
the Holy Spirit.
R. Supreme over all nations, supreme on the earth.

GOSPEL CANTICLE

*(All stand for the Canticle of Mary. Incense may be used
during the singing of the Gospel Canticle.)*

Antiphon

Blessed are those whose way is perfect, who walk in
the law of Yahweh!

Song of the Virgin Mary - Luke 1:46-55

My soul proclaims the greatness of Yahweh,
my spirit rejoices in God my Savior;
for Yahweh has looked with favor on this lowly servant,
and henceforth all generations will call me blessed:

"You, the Almighty, have done great things for me,
and Holy is Your Name.
Your compassion is from generation to generation
to those who revere You.

You have brought victory with Your strength
and have dispersed the arrogant of mind and heart.
You have pulled down the mighty from their thrones
and have raised high the lowly.

You have filled the hungry with good things,
and have dismissed the rich empty handed.

You have come to the help of Israel, Your servant,
remembering Your promise of faithful love,
the promise You made to our ancestors,
to Abraham and to his descendants for ever."

All: Glory to Abba our God, to Christ the Word,
and to the Holy Spirit.
As it was in the beginning,
is now and will be for ever. Amen.

Antiphon

Blessed are those whose way is perfect,
who walk in the law of Yahweh!

INTERCESSIONS

In all that we do, let us praise the name of God, Who
surrounds us with boundless love. In the name of the
Church we pray:
R. Show us Your merciful love, O God.

Be mindful of Your Church through out the world,—
may Your people grow to the fullness of Your love.
R. Show us Your merciful love, O God.

Let all people acknowledge You as the one true
God,—and Jesus Christ, as the Messiah whom You
sent.
R. Show us Your merciful love, O God.

Provide all our neighbors with all they need—so that
they may know Your providence and live in peace.
R. Show us Your merciful love, O God.

Help us to console and support those whose work is
hard and unrewarding—may we work to secure dignity for all workers.
R. Show us Your merciful love, O God.

Show Your mercy and love to all the dead—may
they find their eternal rest and happiness in Your
presence.
R. Show us Your merciful love, O God.

(Other prayers may be added.)

THE ABBA PRAYER OF JESUS

CONCLUDING PRAYER

Almighty and ever faithful God,
source of all that is good,
from the beginning of time You promised us
that You will help us to be always faithful.
Give us grace to serve You with joy,
and know for ever the joy of Your presence
by lives of constant service to those in need.
We ask this in the name of Jesus our Savior.
R. Amen.

BLESSING

May God bless us, protect us from all evil
and bring us to everlasting life.
R. Amen.

GATHERING PRAYERS 2:
Come Before God with Joyful Songs!

INTRODUCTORY VERSE

(All stand and make the sign of the cross as the leader of prayer says:)

    O God, come to my assistance.
    R. Yahweh, make haste to help me.

All: Glory to Abba our God, to Christ the Word,
    and to the Holy Spirit.
    As it was in the beginning,
    is now and will be for ever. Amen.

HYMN

(An appropriate hymn is sung.)

PSALMODY

(During the recitation of the psalms all may sit. Two groups may alternate praying the stanzas of the psalm. The antiphon is prayed by the entire group.)

Psalm 100 A Psalm of Praise to Yahweh, Our Maker.

Antiphon 1
    Come before God with joyful songs!

    Acclaim Yahweh, all the earth!
    Serve Yahweh with gladness!
    Come before God with joyful songs!

    Know that Yahweh is God,
    we belong to Yahweh our Maker,
    we are God's people,
    the sheep of God's pasture.

    Come into God's gates with thanksgiving,
    and to the courts with songs of praise!
    Give thanks and bless God's Name!

    For Yahweh is good;
    Whose faithful love is everlasting,
    Whose faithfulness to all generations.

All: Glory to Abba our God, to Christ the Word,
    and to the Holy Spirit.
    As it was in the beginning,
    is now and will be for ever. Amen.

Antiphon 1

Come before God with joyful songs!\

Silent Prayer

Psalm 119:9-16 God's Law, Our Safeguard from Evil: A Meditative Prayer.

Antiphon 2
    Blessed are You, O Yahweh;
    teach me Your statutes!

    How can the young keep their way pure?
    By guarding it according to Your word.
    I have sought You with my whole heart;
    let me not wander from Your commands!

    I have enclosed Your promise in my heart,
    that I may not sin against You.
    Blessed are You, O Yahweh;
    teach me Your statutes!

    With my lips I have proclaimed
    all the decrees of Your mouth.
    I will rejoice in Your instructions
    more than in all riches.

    I have meditated on Your precepts,
    and am familiar with Your ways.
    I will delight in Your statutes;
    I will not forget Your words.

All: Glory to Abba our God, to Christ the Word,
    and to the Holy Spirit.
    As it was in the beginning,
    is now and will be for ever. Amen.

Antiphon 2
    Blessed are You, O Yahweh;
    teach me Your statutes!

Silent Prayer

READING 1 Thessalonians 3:12-13

(All are seated during the reading.)

May Yahweh God make your love to increase and to overflow towards one another and towards all as our love does towards you. May God make your hearts firm that you may stand before Abba our God, holy and blameless, at the coming of our Lord Jesus Christ with all the saints.

(After the reading a period of silence may be observed followed by a brief shared reflection.)

RESPONSORY
    Claim me once more as Your own, Yahweh.
    R. Come before God with joyful songs!

    Give thanks and bless God's Name,
    R. with joyful songs!

Glory to Abba our God, to Christ the Word, and to the Holy Spirit.
R. Come before God with joyful songs!

GOSPEL CANTICLE

(All stand for the Canticle of Mary. Incense may be used during the singing of the Gospel Canticle.)

Antiphon
I have sought You with my whole heart, O God;
let me not wander from Your commands!

Song of the Virgin Mary - Luke 1:46-55
My soul proclaims the greatness of Yahweh,
my spirit rejoices in God my Savior;
for Yahweh has looked with favor on this lowly servant,
and henceforth all generations will call me blessed:

"You, the Almighty, have done great things for me,
and Holy is Your Name.
Your compassion is from generation to generation
to those who revere You.

You have brought victory with Your strength
and have dispersed the arrogant of mind and heart.
You have pulled down the mighty from their thrones,
and have raised high the lowly.

You have filled the hungry with good things,
and have dismissed the rich empty handed.

You have come to the help of Israel, Your servant,
remembering Your promise of faithful love,
the promise You made to our ancestors,
to Abraham and to his descendants for ever."

All: Glory to Abba our God, to Christ the Word,
and to the Holy Spirit.
As it was in the beginning,
is now and will be for ever. Amen.

Antiphon
I have sought You with my whole heart, O God;
let me not wander from Your commands!

INTERCESSIONS

We join all the earth in giving God, the Most High,
worship and praise. We pray that we may come to
know and believe in God's love for us:
R. Yahweh God, grant us peace.

In Christ You have given us a new covenant—may
we know the greatness which we have inherited.
R. Yahweh God, grant us peace.

Gather into one body all who bear the name Christian—that the world may believe in Christ, whom
You have sent.
R. Yahweh God, grant us peace.

Pour out Your love on all our loved ones—may they
carry with them the gentleness of Christ.
R. Yahweh God, grant us peace.

Show Your love and compassion to those who suffer—may they experience Your comforting love.
R. Yahweh God, grant us peace.

Give peace to those who have died today—in Your
mercy welcome them into Your eternal home.
R. Yahweh God, grant us peace.

(Other prayers may be added.)

THE ABBA PRAYER OF JESUS

CONCLUDING PRAYER

Almighty and ever present God,
ruler of all things in heaven and on earth,
Your watchful care reaches from end to end
and orders all things in Your loving plan.
Listen favorably to the prayers of Your people,
and give us the strength to follow Your call,
so that Your truth may live in our hearts
and reflect peace to those who believe in Your love.
We make this prayer in the name of Jesus our Savior.
R. Amen.

BLESSING

May God bless us, protect us from all evil
and bring us to everlasting life.
R. Amen.

GATHERING PRAYERS 3:
Yahweh Is My Shepherd.

INTRODUCTORY VERSE

(*All stand and make the sign of the cross as the leader of prayer says:*)

    O God, come to my assistance.
    R. Yahweh, make haste to help me.

All: Glory to Abba our God, to Christ the Word,
    and to the Holy Spirit.
    As it was in the beginning,
    is now and will be for ever. Amen.

HYMN

(*An appropriate hymn is sung.*)

PSALMODY

(*During the recitation of the psalms all may sit. wo groups may alternate praying the stanzas of the psalm. The antiphon is prayed by the entire group.*)

Psalm 23 Hymn to Yahweh, the Good Shepherd.

Antiphon 1

    Your goodness and mercy follow me, O God,
    all the days of my life.

    Yahweh is my shepherd,
    shall not want;
    You make me rest in green pastures.
    You lead me beside still waters.

    You restore my spirit.
    You guide me in paths of justice
    for Your Name's sake.

    Even though I walk through the valley
    with shade dark as death,
    I will fear no evil;
    for You are with me;
    Your rod and Your staff,
    they comfort me.

    You prepare a table for me
    in the presence of my enemies;
    You anoint my head with oil;
    my cup runs over.

    Surely Your goodness and mercy
    shall follow me all the days of my life;
    and I shall dwell in Your house
    for all time to come.

All: Glory to Abba our God, to Christ the Word,
    and to the Holy Spirit.

    As it was in the beginning,
    is now and will be for ever. Amen.

Antiphon 1

    Your goodness and mercy follow me, O God,
    all the days of my life.

Silent Prayer

Psalm 119:17-24 God's Law, Our Comfort in Time of Trial: A Meditative Prayer.

Antiphon 2

    I am a sojourner on earth, O God;
    hide not Your commands from me!

    Deal bountifully with Your servant,
    that I may live and observe Your word.
    Open my eyes, that I may behold
    wondrous things out of Your law.

    I am a sojourner on earth;
    hide not Your commands from me!
    My soul is consumed with longing
    for Your decrees in every season.

    You have rebuked the arrogant, the accursed,
    who go astray from Your commands.
    Remove from me reproach and contempt,
    for I have kept Your instructions.

    The ungodly sat and plotted against me,
    but Your servant will meditate on Your statutes.
    Your instructions are my delight,
    Your wishes my counselors.

All: Glory to Abba our God, to Christ the Word,
    and to the Holy Spirit.
    As it was in the beginning,
    is now and will be for ever. Amen.

Antiphon 2

    I am a sojourner on earth, O God;
    hide not Your commands from me!

Silent Prayer

READING 1 John 3:1-3

(*All are seated during the reading.*)

See what love Abba our God has bestowed on us, in letting us be called children of God; and that is what we really are! The reason why the world does not recognize us is that it never recognized God. Beloved, we are the children of God right now; and what we shall be, has not yet been revealed. But we know, that at this revelation, we shall be like God, for we shall see God as God really is. All who have this hope based on God make themselves pure even as Christ is pure.

(After the reading a period of silence may be observed followed by a brief shared reflection.)

RESPONSORY

Yahweh, all You ask of me is truth.
R. In the depths of my heart teach me wisdom of heart.

You guide me in paths of justice,
R. teach me wisdom of heart.

Glory to Abba our God, to Christ the Word,
and to the Holy Spirit.
R. In the depths of my heart teach me wisdom of heart.

GOSPEL CANTICLE

(All stand for the Canticle of Mary. Incense may be used during the singing of the Gospel Canticle.)

Antiphon

Your instructions are my delight, O Yahweh.

Song of the Virgin Mary - Luke 1:46-55

My soul proclaims the greatness of Yahweh,
my spirit rejoices in God my Savior;
for Yahweh has looked with favor on this lowly servant,
and henceforth all generations will call me blessed:

"You, the Almighty, have done great things for me,
and Holy is Your Name.
Your compassion is from generation to generation
to those who revere You.

You have brought victory with Your strength
and have dispersed the arrogant of mind and heart.
You have pulled down the mighty from their thrones,
and have raised high the lowly.

You have filled the hungry with good things,
and have dismissed the rich empty handed.

You have come to the help of Israel, Your servant,
remembering Your promise of faithful love,
the promise You made to our ancestors,
to Abraham and to his descendants for ever."

All: Glory to Abba our God, to Christ the Word,
and to the Holy Spirit.
As it was in the beginning,
is now and will be for ever. Amen.

Antiphon

Your instructions are my delight, O Yahweh.

INTERCESSIONS

Sing a new song to Yahweh! Sing to Yahweh, all the earth. With gladness and joy as we pray:
R. Abba our God, grant us unity and peace.

Source of all authority, guide all leaders and heads of the nations—give them wisdom and integrity to pursue the good of all.
R. Abba our God, grant us unity and peace.

You are the source of all freedom—grant freedom to those in captivity of mind or body.
R. Abba our God, grant us unity and peace.

Give courage and strength to our young people—may they remain blameless in Your sight and generously follow Your call.
R. Abba our God, grant us unity and peace.

May young people follow Christ the light of the world—and grow in wisdom and grace.
R. Abba our God, grant us unity and peace.

Receive our dead brothers and sisters into Your eternal reign—sustain our hope to reign with You for ever.
R. Abba our God, grant us unity and peace.

(Other prayers may be added.)

THE ABBA PRAYER OF JESUS

CONCLUDING PRAYER

All powerful and ever living God,
the love You offer us always exceeds
the furthest expression of our human longing.
Guide each thought, each effort of our life,
and direct our steps in the way of Your love,
that our efforts in the name of Jesus
may bring humankind to unity and peace.
We make this prayer in the name of Jesus our Savior.
R. Amen.

BLESSING

May God bless us, protect us from all evil
and bring us to everlasting life.
R. Amen.

GATHERING PRAYERS
I Will Meditate on Your Won᷉ ᷉orks.

INTRODUCTORY VERSE

(*All stand and make the sign of the cross as the leader of prayer says:*)
> O God, come to my assistance.
> **R.** Yahweh, make haste to help me.

All: Glory to Abba our God, to Christ the Word,
and to the Holy Spirit.
As it was in the beginning,
is now and will be for ever. Amen.

HYMN

(*An appropriate hymn is sung.*)

PSALMODY

(*During the recitation of the psalms all may sit. Two groups may alternate praying the stanzas of the psalm. The antiphon is prayed by the entire group.*)

Psalm 84:1-4,12 Desire for God's Sanctuary

Antiphon 1
> Blessed are those who trust in You, O God!

> How lovely is Your dwelling,
> O Yahweh Sabaoth!

> My whole being longs and pines
> for Your courts, O Yahweh!
> My heart and flesh shout for joy
> to You, O living God!

> Even the sparrow has found a home,
> the swallow a nest to place its young:
> Your altars, Yahweh Sabaoth,
> Adonai and my God!

> Blessed are they who dwell in Your house,
> they shall always sing Your praises!
> O Yahweh Sabaoth,
> blessed are those who trust in You!

All: Glory to Abba our God, to Christ the Word,
and to the Holy Spirit.
As it was in the beginning,
is now and will be for ever. Amen.

Antiphon 1
> Blessed are those who trust in You, O God!

Silent Prayer

Psalm 119:25-32 God's Law, Our Help in Distress: A Meditative Prayer.

Antiphon 2
> Make me understand the way of Your precepts,
> and I will meditate on Your wondrous works.

> I lie prostrate in the dust;
> revive me according to Your word!
> I have recounted my ways and You heard me;
> teach me Your statutes!

> Make me understand the way of Your precepts,
> and I will meditate on Your wondrous works.
> My soul melts away with grief;
> raise me according to Your word!

> Remove from me the way of lying;
> and graciously teach me Your law!
> I have chosen the way of truth,
> I set Your decrees before me.

> I have clung to Your instructions,
> O Yahweh, do not put me to shame!
> I will run the way of Your commands
> if You enlarge my understanding!

All: Glory to Abba our God, to Christ the Word,
and to the Holy Spirit.
As it was in the beginning,
is now and will be for ever. Amen.

Antiphon 2
> Make me understand the way of Your precepts,
> and I will meditate on Your wondrous works.

Silent Prayer

READING James 1:19-22,25

(*All are seated during the reading.*)

Of this you may be certain, my friends. Everyone should be quick to listen but slow to speak and slow to be angry. For human anger cannot further the justice of God. Do away with all impurities and remnants of evil. In meekness welcome the Word that has been planted in you and is able to save your souls. Become doers of the Word, and not merely hearers, who deceive themselves. But those who look into the perfect law, the law of liberty, and continue in it, and since they are not forgetful hearers but put it into practice, they will be blessed in their every undertaking.

(*After the reading a period of silence may be observed followed by a brief shared reflection.*)

RESPONSORY

Yahweh, show me Your ways.
R. Teach me to walk in Your footsteps.

My heart shout for joy to You,
R. to walk in Your footsteps.

Glory to Abba our God, to Christ the Word, and to the Holy Spirit.
R. Teach me to walk in Your footsteps.

GOSPEL CANTICLE

(All stand for the Canticle of Mary. Incense may be used during the singing of the Gospel Canticle.)

Antiphon

I have chosen the way of truth,
I set Your decrees before me, O God.

Song of the Virgin Mary - Luke 1:46-55

My soul proclaims the greatness of Yahweh,
my spirit rejoices in God my Savior;
for Yahweh has looked with favor on this lowly servant,
and henceforth all generations will call me blessed:

"You, the Almighty, have done great things for me,
and Holy is Your Name.
Your compassion is from generation to generation
to those who revere You.

You have brought victory with Your strength
and have dispersed the arrogant of mind and heart.
You have pulled down the mighty from their thrones,
and have raised high the lowly.

You have filled the hungry with good things,
and have dismissed the rich empty handed.

You have come to the help of Israel, Your servant,
remembering Your promise of faithful love,
the promise You made to our ancestors,
to Abraham and to his descendants for ever."

All: Glory to Abba our God, to Christ the Word,
and to the Holy Spirit.
As it was in the beginning,
is now and will be for ever. Amen.

Antiphon

I have chosen the way of truth,
I set Your decrees before me, O God.

INTERCESSIONS

Save us, Yahweh our God, and gather us together
from the nations, that we may proclaim Your holy
name and glory in Your praise.
R. Abba our God, fill us by Your love.

Yahweh God, source of all goodness, bring justice to
our world—make us always mindful of the marvelous deeds You have done.
R. Abba our God, fill us by Your love.

Lead people everywhere to the joy of Your eternal
reign—may they give tireless and faithful witness to
Your Gospel.
R. Abba our God, fill us by Your love.

Reward all those who have done good to us—may
they live in the joy of Your peace.
R. Abba our God, fill us by Your love.

May Your Spirit enter the hearts of all, especially of
those in public office—and may their eyes turn with
compassion to those oppressed with poverty and
injustice.
R. Abba our God, fill us by Your love.

Give to the married people the strength of Your
peace, the guidance of Your will—and the grace to
live together in constant love.
R. Abba our God, fill us by Your love.

(Other prayers may be added.)

THE ABBA PRAYER OF JESUS

CONCLUDING PRAYER

Living and ever creating God,
You formed us from the very beginning of time,
in Your own likeness and image.
Bless us with greater love for You,
and for our brothers and sisters.
May we serve You with our every desire
and show love for one another
with a love that is worthy of You.
We ask this through Christ our Savior.
R. Amen.

BLESSING

May God bless us, protect us from all evil and bring
us to everlasting life.
R. Amen.

GATHERING PRAYERS 5:

Incline My Heart to Your Instructions.

INTRODUCTORY VERSE

(All stand and make the sign of the cross as the leader of prayer says:)

    O God, come to my assistance.
    R. Yahweh, make haste to help me.

All: Glory to Abba our God, to Christ the Word,
    and to the Holy Spirit.
    As it was in the beginning,
    is now and will be for ever. Amen.

HYMN

(An appropriate hymn is sung.)

PSALMODY

(During the recitation of the psalms all may sit. Two groups may alternate praying the stanzas of the psalm. The antiphon is prayed by the entire group.)

Psalm 67 Harvest Song of Blessing.

Antiphon 1

    Let the peoples thank You, O God;
    let all the peoples thank You!

    God, be gracious to us and bless us
    and make Your face to shine upon us,
    that Your ways may be known upon earth,
    Your saving power among all nations.

    Let the peoples thank You, O God;
    let all the peoples thank You!

    Let the nations be glad and sing for joy,
    for You judge the peoples with justice
    and govern the nations on earth.

    Let the peoples thank You, O God;
    let all the peoples thank You!

    May the earth yield its produce,
    may God, our God, bless us.
    May God continue to bless us;
    and be revered to the ends of the earth.

All: Glory to Abba our God, to Christ the Word,
    and to the Holy Spirit.
    As it was in the beginning,
    is now and will be for ever. Amen.

Antiphon 1

    Let the peoples thank You, O God;
    let all the peoples thank You!

Silent Prayer

Psalm 119:33-40 God's Law, Our Source of Wisdom: A Meditative Prayer.

Antiphon 2

    Direct me in the path of Your commands,
    for my delight is in Your precepts, O God.

    Teach me, O Yahweh, the way of Your statutes;
    and I will keep it to the end.
    Give me understanding, that I may keep Your law
    and observe it with my whole heart.

    Direct me in the path of Your commands,
    for my delight is therein.
    Incline my heart to Your instructions,
    and not to unjust gain!

    Turn my eyes from looking at vanities;
    and restore my life in Your ways.
    Confirm Your promise to Your servant,
    who is faithful in revering You.

    Remove the reproach because I revere You;
    for Your decrees are good.
    See how I yearn for Your precepts;
    in Your saving justice give me life!

All: Glory to Abba our God, to Christ the Word,
    and to the Holy Spirit.
    As it was in the beginning,
    is now and will be for ever. Amen.

Antiphon 2

    Direct me in the path of Your commands,
    for my delight is in Your precepts, O God.

Silent Prayer

READING Ephesians 4:29-32

(All are seated during the reading.)

Let no foul word proceed from your mouth. Let your words be for the improvement of others, as fits the occasion, that they may impart grace to the hearers. Do not grieve the Holy Spirit of God, by Whom you were sealed for the day of redemption.

Let all harshness, wrath, anger, clamor, and slander be put away from you, along with malice of every sort. Be kind and tenderhearted to one another, forgiving one another, just as God forgave you in Christ.

(After the reading a period of silence may be observed followed by a brief shared reflection.)

RESPONSORY

Give me understanding, that I may keep Your law.
R. Teach me, O Yahweh, the way of Your statutes.

Confirm Your promise to Your servant,
R. the way of Your statutes.

Glory to Abba our God, to Christ the Word,
and to the Holy Spirit.
R. Teach me, O Yahweh, the way of Your statutes.

GOSPEL CANTICLE

(All stand for the Canticle of Mary. Incense may be used during the singing of the Gospel Canticle.)

Antiphon

Turn my eyes from looking at vanities, O God;
and restore my life in Your ways.

Song of the Virgin Mary - Luke 1:46-55

My soul proclaims the greatness of Yahweh,
my spirit rejoices in God my Savior;
for Yahweh has looked with favor on this lowly servant,
and henceforth all generations will call me blessed:

"You, the Almighty, have done great things for me,
and Holy is Your Name.
Your compassion is from generation to generation
to those who revere You.
You have brought victory with Your strength
and have dispersed the arrogant of mind and heart.
You have pulled down the mighty from their thrones,
and have raised high the lowly.

You have filled the hungry with good things,
and have dismissed the rich empty handed.

You have come to the help of Israel, Your servant,
remembering Your promise of faithful love,
the promise You made to our ancestors,
to Abraham and to his descendants for ever."

All: Glory to Abba our God, to Christ the Word,
and to the Holy Spirit.
As it was in the beginning,
is now and will be for ever. Amen.

Antiphon

Turn my eyes from looking at vanities, O God;
and restore my life in Your ways.

INTERCESSIONS

Come, let us worship Yahweh, our God! Let us bow down in the presence of Yahweh, our Maker, and pray:
R. Abba God, guard us with Your constant love.

Guide our thoughts, our words and actions—that all we do today may be pleasing to You.
R. Abba God, guard us with Your constant love.

Help us to avoid all that is displeasing to You—show us Your mercy and loving-kindness.
R. Abba God, guard us with Your constant love.

Through the passion, the death and the resurrection of Christ, You have given us new life—give us the strength of Your Holy Spirit.
R. Abba God, guard us with Your constant love.

Look with favor on those who trust in our prayers—and give them all they need for body and soul.
R. Abba God, guard us with Your constant love.

(Other prayers may be added.)

THE ABBA PRAYER OF JESUS

CONCLUDING PRAYER

Bowing down in the presence of Yahweh, our maker,
we pray You in faith and love, our living God,
to guard Your family gathered here.
In You mercy and loving kindness
may no thought of ours be left unguarded,
no tear unheeded, no joy unnoticed.
May the blessings promised to the poor in Spirit
and those who hunger and thirst for what is right,
be ours in Your heavenly reign.
We ask this through Christ our Savior.
R. Amen.

BLESSING

May God bless us, protect us from all evil
and bring us to everlasting life.
R. Amen.

GATHERING PRAYERS 6:
Sing to Yahweh A New Song.

INTRODUCTORY VERSE

(All stand and make the sign of the cross as the leader of prayer says:)

O God, come to my assistance.
R. Yahweh, make haste to help me.

All: Glory to Abba our God, to Christ the Word,
and to the Holy Spirit.
As it was in the beginning,
is now and will be for ever. Amen.

HYMN

(An appropriate hymn is sung.)

PSALMODY

(During the recitation of the psalms all may sit. Two groups may alternate praying the stanzas of the psalm. The antiphon is prayed by the entire group.)

Psalm 149 Hymn to Celebrate the Justice of Yahweh

Antiphon 1

Praise Yahweh, Alleluia!

Sing to Yahweh a new song,
sing praise in the assembly of the faithful!
Let Israel rejoice in their Maker,
let the children of Zion delight in their Ruler!

Let them praise the Name with dancing,
let them sing praise to God with timbrel and
For Yahweh loves the chosen people;
and crowns the humble with victory.

Let the faithful exult in their Glorious One,
let them sing for joy on their couches.
Let the high praises of God be in their throats,
to give glory for all the saints.

All: Glory to Abba our God, to Christ the Word,
and to the Holy Spirit.
As it was in the beginning,
is now and will be for ever. Amen.

Antiphon 1

Praise Yahweh, Alleluia!

Silent Prayer

Psalm 119:41-48 God's Law, Our Source of Courage: A Meditative Prayer.

Antiphon 2

Remove not the word of truth out of my mouth,
for my hope is in Your decrees, O God.

Let Your faithful love come to me, Yahweh,
save me according to Your promise.
Give me an answer to those who provoke me,
for I trust in Your word.

Remove not the word of truth out of my mouth,
for my hope is in Your decrees.
I will keep Your law without fail,
for ever and ever.

I shall live in all freedom,
for I have sought Your precepts.
I shall speak of Your instructions before rulers,
and will not be ashamed.

I find delight in Your commands,
I love them dearly.
I revere Your commands, which I love,
and I will meditate on Your statutes.

All: Glory to Abba our God, to Christ the Word,
and to the Holy Spirit.
As it was in the beginning,
is now and will be for ever. Amen.

Antiphon 2

Remove not the word of truth out of my mouth,
for my hope is in Your decrees, O God.

Silent Prayer

READING 2 Peter 1:10-11

(All are seated during the reading.)

On account of this, brothers and sisters, be solicitous to confirm your call and election, for if you do this there will be no danger of your stumbling. For in this way you will be given the generous gift of entrance into the eternal Realm of our Lord and Savior Jesus Christ.

(After the reading a period of silence may be observed followed by a brief shared reflection.)

RESPONSORY

Let the faithful exult in their Glorious One.
R. Yahweh, our God, is tender and compassionate.

Yahweh, our God, is patient and ready to forgive,
R. tender and compassionate.

Glory to Abba our God, to Christ the Word, and to the Holy Spirit.
R. Yahweh, our God, is tender and compassionate.

GOSPEL CANTICLE

(*All stand for the Canticle of Mary. Incense may be used during the singing of the Gospel Canticle.*)

Antiphon

I revere Your commands, O Yahweh,
and I will meditate on Your statutes.

Song of the Virgin Mary - Luke 1:46-55

My soul proclaims the greatness of Yahweh,
my spirit rejoices in God my Savior;
for Yahweh has looked with favor on this lowly servant,
and henceforth all generations will call me blessed:

"You, the Almighty, have done great things for me,
and Holy is Your Name.
Your compassion is from generation to generation
to those who revere You.

You have brought victory with Your strength
and have dispersed the arrogant of mind and heart.
You have pulled down the mighty from their throne
and have raised high the lowly.

You have filled the hungry with good things,
and have dismissed the rich empty handed.

You have come to the help of Israel, Your servant,
remembering Your promise of faithful love,
the promise You made to our ancestors,
to Abraham and to his descendants for ever."

All: Glory to Abba our God, to Christ the Word,
and to the Holy Spirit.
As it was in the beginning,
is now and will be for ever. Amen.

Antiphon

I revere Your commands, O Yahweh,
and I will meditate on Your statutes.

INTERCESSIONS

Yahweh our God, You are our Rock of safety, and our Stronghold. For the honor of Your name, lead me and guide me in Your ways.
R. Guide us by Your law of love.

You filled us with Your light in baptism—may we dedicate and consecrate this day to You.
R. Guide us by Your law of love.

May we give You praise every day and at every hour of the day—may we take Your word with us wherever we go.
R. Guide us by Your law of love.

Control our thoughts, words and deeds—so that our lives may prove acceptable to You today.
R. Guide us by Your law of love.

We pray for all those whom we have already met and will meet today—bless them, their relatives and their friends.
R. Guide us by Your law of love.

(*Other prayers may be added.*)

THE ABBA PRAYER OF JESUS

CONCLUDING PRAYER

Yahweh God, our rock of safety and stronghold,
You have promised to remain forever
with those who do what is just and right.
Help us to live constantly in Your presence,
do everything guided by Your law of love,
and bring Your salvation to the ends of the earth.
We ask this through Christ our Savior.
R. Amen.

BLESSING

May God bless us, protect us from all evil
and bring us to everlasting life.
R. Amen.

GATHERING PRAYERS 7:

Sing Joyfully to Yahweh, All the Earth.

INTRODUCTORY VERSE

(*All stand and make the sign of the cross as the leader of prayer says:*)

O God, come to my assistance.
R. Yahweh, make haste to help me.

All: Glory to Abba our God, to Christ the Word,
and to the Holy Spirit.
As it was in the beginning,
is now and will be for ever. Amen.

HYMN

(*An appropriate hymn is sung.*)

PSALMODY

(*During the recitation of the psalms all may sit. Two groups may alternate praying the stanzas of the psalm. The antiphon is prayed by the entire group.*)

Psalm 98 A Hymn praising Yahweh's Eternal Rule

Antiphon 1

Sing joyfully to Yahweh, all the earth.
Sing a new song to Yahweh,
Who has done marvelous things!
In Whose right hand,
in Whose holy arm is saving power.

Yahweh, You have made known Your victory,
You have revealed Your justice for all to see.
You have remembered Your faithful love
and constancy to the house of Israel.

All the ends of the earth have seen
the saving power of our God.
Sing joyfully to Yahweh, all the earth;
break forth into joyous song and sing praises!

Sing praises to Yahweh with the lyre,
with the lyre and the sound of melody!
With trumpets and the sound of the horn
sing joyfully before Yahweh the Ruler!

Let the sea roar, and all that fills it,
the world and those who dwell in it!
Let the floods clap their hands,
let the hills sing for joy together.

All: Glory to Abba our God, to Christ the Word,
and to the Holy Spirit.
As it was in the beginning,
is now and will be for ever. Amen.

Antiphon 1

Sing joyfully to Yahweh, all the earth.

Silent Prayer

Psalm 119:49-56 God's Law, Our Source of Consolation: A Meditative Prayer.

Antiphon 2

I remember Your decrees of old and I am comforted.
Remember Your word to Your servant,
upon which You made me rest my hope.
This is my comfort in my affliction
that Your promises restored me to life.

The arrogant ridiculed me incessantly
but I have not strayed from Your law.
I have remembered Your decrees of old,
truly, O Yahweh, I am comforted.

Fury grips me when I see the wicked
who abandon Your law.
Your statutes have been my songs
in the house of my pilgrimage.

All night I have remembered Your Name,
and have observed Your law, O Yahweh.
This has been my practice,
and I have kept Your precepts.

All: Glory to Abba our God, to Christ the Word,
and to the Holy Spirit.
As it was in the beginning,
is now and will be for ever. Amen.

Antiphon 2

I remember Your decrees of old and I am comforted.

Silent Prayer

READING Colossians 1:2-6

(*All are seated during the reading.*)

May Abba our God give you grace and peace. We thank God, the Abba of our Savior Jesus Christ, as we pray for you at all times. For we have heard of your faith in Christ Jesus and of your love for all God's people on account of the hope which is laid up for you in heaven. You have already heard of this hope in the Word of truth, the gospel which came to you in the same way, as indeed it is bearing fruit and growing in the whole world.

(After the reading a period of silence may be observed followed by a brief shared reflection.)

RESPONSORY

Sing joyfully to Yahweh, all the earth.
R. O Yahweh, how wonderful are Your works.

Remember Your word to Your servant,
R. how wonderful are Your works.

Glory to Abba our God, to Christ the Word,
and to the Holy Spirit.
R. O Yahweh, how wonderful are Your works.

GOSPEL CANTICLE

(All stand for the Canticle of Mary. Incense may be used during the singing of the Gospel Canticle.)

Antiphon

Remember Your word to Your servant, O God.

Song of the Virgin Mary - Luke 1:46-55

My soul proclaims the greatness of Yahweh,
my spirit rejoices in God my Savior;
for Yahweh has looked with favor on this lowly servant, and henceforth all generations will call me blessed:

"You, the Almighty, have done great things for me,
and Holy is Your Name.
Your compassion is from generation to generation
to those who revere You.

You have brought victory with Your strength
and have dispersed the arrogant of mind and heart.
You have pulled down the mighty from their thrones,
and have raised high the lowly.

You have filled the hungry with good things,
and have dismissed the rich empty handed.

You have come to the help of Israel, Your servant,
remembering Your promise of faithful love,
he promise You made to our ancestors,
to Abraham and to his descendants for ever."

All: Glory to Abba our God, to Christ the Word,
and to the Holy Spirit.
As it was in the beginning,
is now and will be for ever. Amen.

Antiphon

Remember Your word to Your servant, O God.

INTERCESSIONS

Yahweh, Your mercy is our hope, our hearts rejoice
in Your saving power. We will sing to You, Yahweh
for Your goodness to us. With joy we pray:
R. Yahweh God, we trust in You.

We pray for N., our Pope, and N., our bishop—guide
them and bless them in their work.
R. Yahweh God, we trust in You

May the sick share their sufferings with Christ—and
may they find in Christ fullness of life and love.
R. Yahweh God, we trust in You

Have compassion on those who have nowhere to lay
their head—make us aware of the needs of the homeless.
R. Yahweh God, we trust in You

Bless and reward those who work on the land—ay
we accept the fruits of the earth with gratitude.
R. Yahweh God, we trust in You.

Look with compassion on those who have died as a
result of war, violence and hatred—welcome them
into Your presence and give them peace.
R. Yahweh God, we trust in You.

(Other prayers may be added.)

THE ABBA PRAYER OF JESUS

CONCLUDING PRAYER

God of power and might
faith in Your word is the way to wisdom,
and trust in Your divine plan is to grow in truth.
Grant that with our thoughts always fixed on You
we may please You in all that we say and do.
Open our eyes to Your deeds,
our ears to the sound of Your call,
and make us more like Jesus Christ,
who lives and reigns with You and the Holy Spirit,
one God, for ever and ever.
R. Amen.

BLESSING

May God bless us, protect us from all evil
and bring us to everlasting life.
R. Amen.

GATHERING PRAYERS 8:

Blessed Be the Name of Yahweh

INTRODUCTORY VERSE

(*All stand and make the sign of the cross as the leader of prayer says:*)

    O God, come to my assistance.
    R. Yahweh, make haste to help me.

All: Glory to Abba our God, to Christ the Word,
    and to the Holy Spirit.
    As it was in the beginning,
    is now and will be for ever. Amen.

HYMN

(*An appropriate hymn is sung.*)

PSALMODY

(*During the recitation of the psalms all may sit. Two groups may alternate praying the stanzas of the psalm. The antiphon is prayed by the entire group.*)

Psalm 113 Hymn to Yahweh's Mercy and Compassion

Antiphon 1
    Blessed be the Name of Yahweh
    henceforth and for evermore!

    Praise, O servants of Yahweh,
    praise the Name of Yahweh!
    Blessed be the Name of Yahweh
    henceforth and for evermore!

    From the rising of the sun to its setting,
    praised be the Name of Yahweh!
    Yahweh is high above all nations,
    whose glory is above the heavens!

    Who is like Yahweh our God,
    whose throne is set on high,
    but Who stoops to look down
    on the heavens and the earth?

    Yahweh raises the poor from the dust,
    and lifts the needy out of the dunghill,
    to make them sit with the nobles,
    with the nobles of the chosen people.

    Yahweh gives the childless woman a family,
    making her the joyful mother of children.
    Praise Yahweh!

All: Glory to Abba our God, to Christ the Word,
    and to the Holy Spirit.
    As it was in the beginning,
    is now and will be for ever. Amen.

Antiphon 1
    Blessed be the Name of Yahweh
    henceforth and for evermore!

Silent Prayer

Psalm 119:57-64 God's Law, Our Source of Devotion: A Meditative Prayer.

Antiphon 2
    Be gracious to me according to Your promise.

    You are my portion, O Yahweh,
    I promise to observe Your word.
    I entreat Your favor with all my heart;
    be gracious to me according to Your promise.

    I considered Your ways,
    I turn my steps to Your instructions.
    I hastened and did not delay
    to observe Your commands.

    Though the wicked encircled me,
    I did not forget Your law.
    At midnight I rise to praise You,
    because of Your just decrees.

    I am a companion of all who revere You,
    of all who observe Your precepts.
    The earth, is full of Your faithful love;
    O Yahweh, teach me Your statutes!

All: Glory to Abba our God, to Christ the Word,
    and to the Holy Spirit.
    As it was in the beginning,
    is now and will be for ever. Amen.

Antiphon 2
    Be gracious to me according to Your promise.

Silent Prayer

READING 2 Thessalonians 2:13-14

(*All are seated during the reading.*)

We must always give thanks to God for you, brothers and sisters whom God loves, because God chose you from the beginning to be saved by the Spirit who makes us holy, and through faith in the truth. God called you for this purpose through our proclamation of the Good News that you might share in the glory of our Lord Jesus Christ.

(After the reading a period of silence may be observed followed by a brief shared reflection.)

RESPONSORY

I will sing for ever of Your mercy, O Yahweh.
R. I will make known to all generations Your faithful-love, O God.

At midnight I rise to praise You,
R. Your faithful-love, O God.

Glory to Abba our God, to Christ the Word, and to the Holy Spirit.
R. I will make known to all generations Your faithful-love, O God.

GOSPEL CANTICLE

(All stand for the Canticle of Mary. Incense may be used during the singing of the Gospel Canticle.)

Antiphon

The earth, is full of Your faithful love;
O Yahweh, teach me Your statutes!

Song of the Virgin Mary - Luke 1:46-55

My soul proclaims the greatness of Yahweh,
my spirit rejoices in God my Savior;
for Yahweh has looked with favor on this lowly servant,
and henceforth all generations will call me blessed:

"You, the Almighty, have done great things for me,
and Holy is Your Name.
Your compassion is from generation to generation
to those who revere You.

You have brought victory with Your strength
and have dispersed the arrogant of mind and heart.
You have pulled down the mighty from their thrones,
and have raised high the lowly.

You have filled the hungry with good things,
and have dismissed the rich empty handed.

You have come to the help of Israel, Your servant,
remembering Your promise of faithful love,
the promise You made to our ancestors,
to Abraham and to his descendants for ever."

All: Glory to Abba our God, to Christ the Word,
and to the Holy Spirit.
As it was in the beginning,
is now and will be for ever. Amen.

Antiphon

The earth, is full of Your faithful love;
O Yahweh, teach me Your statutes!

INTERCESSIONS

Yahweh, our strength, leads us into freedom and salvation. Let us sing the name of Yahweh, Most High. Sustained by our faith we pray:
R. Remember Your people O God.

We pray for all the people of the world that they may seek the way that leads to peace—that human rights and freedom may be respected everywhere, and that the world's resources may be generously shared.
R. Remember Your people O God.

We pray for the Church—that the Church leaders may be faithful ministers of Your word, and that all members may be strong in faith and hope.
R. Remember Your people O God.

We pray for the families and the community in which we live—may we find Your presence in them.
R. Remember Your people O God.

We pray for those who travel—may they enjoy peace and well-being and reach their destination in safety and joy.
R. Remember Your people O God.

We pray for the faithful departed—may they rest in peace through Your mercy.

(Other prayers may be added.)

THE ABBA PRAYER OF JESUS

CONCLUDING PRAYER

God of providence,
form in us the likeness of Christ, Your Word,
and deepen Your life within us.
Guide the course of world events,
bring peace to the world
and freedom to the Church,
that Christ may find welcome in the world.
Touch the hearts of all people with Your love
that they in turn may love one another.
We ask this through Christ our Savior.
R. Amen.

BLESSING

May God bless us, protect us from all evil
and bring us to everlasting life.
R. Amen.

16

GATHERING PRAYERS 9:
Praise God for Sovereign Majesty!

INTRODUCTORY VERSE

(All stand and make the sign of the cross as the leader of prayer says:)

O God, come to my assistance.
R. Yahweh, make haste to help me.

All: Glory to Abba our God, to Christ the Word,
and to the Holy Spirit.
As it was in the beginning,
is now and will be for ever. Amen.

HYMN

(An appropriate hymn is sung.)

PSALMODY

(During the recitation of the psalms all may sit. Two groups may alternate praying the stanzas of the psalm. The antiphon is prayed by the entire group.)

Psalm 150 Hymn to the Creator: A Doxology

Antiphon 1

Alleluia! Praise Yahweh!
Praise God with songs of praise!

Praise Yahweh in the holy places;
praise God in the mighty firmament!
Praise Yahweh for mighty deeds;
praise God for sovereign majesty!

Praise Yahweh with trumpet sound;
praise God with harp and lyre!
Praise Yahweh with tambourines and dancing;
praise God with strings and pipes!

Praise Yahweh with clashing cymbals,
praise God with triumphant cymbals!
Let everything that breathes praise Yahweh!
Praise Yahweh! Alleluia!

All: Glory to Abba our God, to Christ the Word,
and to the Holy Spirit.
As it was in the beginning,
is now and will be for ever. Amen.

Antiphon 1

Alleluia! Praise Yahweh!
Praise God with songs of praise!

Silent Prayer

Psalm 119:65-72 God's Law, Our Source of Goodness: A Meditative Prayer.

Antiphon 2

Teach me good judgment and knowledge, O Yahweh,

for I believe in Your commands.
You have dealt well with Your servant,
O Yahweh, according to Your word.
Teach me good judgment and knowledge,
for I believe in Your commands.

Before I was humbled I used to go astray,
but now I keep Your promise.
You are good and the cause of good;
teach me Your statutes.

The arrogant besmear me with lies,
but I observe Your precepts with all my heart.
Their heart is like fat without feeling
but I delight in Your law.

It was good for me that I was humbled,
that I might learn Your statutes.
More precious to me is the law from Your mouth,
than thousands of gold and silver pieces.

All: Glory to Abba our God, to Christ the Word,
and to the Holy Spirit.
As it was in the beginning,
is now and will be for ever. Amen.

Antiphon 2

Teach me good judgment and knowledge, O Yahweh,
for I believe in Your commands.

Silent Prayer

READING Ezekiel 36:25-28

(All are seated during the reading.)

I will pour clean water over you, and you shall be clean. I will cleanse you from all your impurities, and from all your foul idols. I will also give you a new heart, and I will put a new spirit within you. I will remove the stony heart from your body and give you a heart of flesh instead. I will put my Spirit within you, and make you conform to my statutes, keep my laws and live by them. You shall live in the land which I gave to your ancestors. You shall be a people to Me and I will be God to you.

(After the reading a period of silence may be observed followed by a brief shared reflection.)

RESPONSORY

Create a clean heart for me, O God.
R. Remove the stony heart and give me a new heart.

Do not cast me away from Your presence,
R. and give me a new heart.

Glory to Abba our God, to Christ the Word,
and to the Holy Spirit.
R. Remove the stony heart and give me a new heart.

GOSPEL CANTICLE

(*All stand for the Canticle of Mary. Incense may be used during the singing of the Gospel Canticle.*)

Antiphon

You are good and the cause of good;
teach me Your statutes, O Yahweh.

Song of the Virgin Mary - Luke 1:46-55

My soul proclaims the greatness of Yahweh,
my spirit rejoices in God my Savior;
for Yahweh has looked with favor on this lowly servant,
and henceforth all generations will call me blessed:

"You, the Almighty, have done great things for me,
and Holy is Your Name.
Your compassion is from generation to generation
to those who revere You.

You have brought victory with Your strength
and have dispersed the arrogant of mind and heart.
You have pulled down the mighty from their thrones,
and have raised high the lowly.

You have filled the hungry with good things,
and have dismissed the rich empty handed.

You have come to the help of Israel, Your servant,
remembering Your promise of faithful love,
the promise You made to our ancestors,
to Abraham and to his descendants for ever."

All: Glory to Abba our God, to Christ the Word,
and to the Holy Spirit.
As it was in the beginning,
is now and will be for ever. Amen.

Antiphon

You are good and the cause of good;
teach me Your statutes, O Yahweh.

INTERCESSIONS

When we call upon You, Yahweh our God, You always answer us and bend Your ear and hear our prayer. With trust, joy and gratitude we pray:
R. We praise You, O God, and we thank You.

We welcome You into our hearts with praise and gratitude—may our vision be always fixed on You.
R. We praise You, O God, and we thank You.

Show us Your goodness this day—and open our eyes and our hearts to Your love in the world.
R. We praise You, O God, and we thank You.

We will praise You in our words and actions today—and help to overcome evil with good.
R. We praise You, O God, and we thank You.

We pray for all Christian families—may Your Spirit deepen their unity in love and faith.
R. We praise You, O God, and we thank You.

You were anointed by Your Spirit—may we listen to Your Spirit who lives in us.
R. We praise You, O God, and we thank You.

(*Other prayers may be added.*)

THE ABBA PRAYER OF JESUS

CONCLUDING PRAYER

Yahweh, our God,
You govern us with unfailing wisdom
and surround us with compassionate love.
Increase our faith and hope in You,
teach us to cherish the gifts that surround us,
and bring our trust to its promised fulfillment
in the joy and peace of Your eternal reign.
We ask this through Christ our Savior.
R. Amen.

BLESSING

May God bless us, protect us from all evil
and bring us to everlasting life.
R. Amen.

GATHERING PRAYERS 10:
Let Your Faithful Love be My Comfort.

INTRODUCTORY VERSE

(*All stand and make the sign of the cross as the leader of prayer says:*)

O God, come to my assistance.

R. Yahweh, make haste to help me.

All: Glory to Abba our God, to Christ the Word,
and to the Holy Spirit.
As it was in the beginning,
is now and will be for ever. Amen.

HYMN

(*An appropriate hymn is sung.*)

PSALMODY

(*During the recitation of the psalms all may sit. Two groups may alternate praying the stanzas of the psalm. The antiphon is prayed by the entire group.*)

Psalm 134 Come Bless Yahweh at Night

Antiphon 1

Lift up your hands to the sanctuary,
and bless Yahweh, our God!

Come, bless Yahweh,
all you who serve Yahweh,
who stand in the house of Yahweh,
through the watches of the night.

Lift up your hands to the sanctuary,
and bless Yahweh!
May Yahweh bless you from Zion,
the Maker of the heavens and the earth!

All: Glory to Abba our God, to Christ the Word,
and to the Holy Spirit.
As it was in the beginning,
is now and will be for ever. Amen.

Antiphon 1

Lift up your hands to the sanctuary,
and bless Yahweh, our God!

Silent Prayer

Psalm 119:73-80 God's Law, Our Source of Justice: A Meditative Prayer.

Antiphon 2

Those who revere You shall see me and rejoice,
because I have hoped in Your word, O God.

Your hands have made me and fashioned me;
give me insight that I may learn Your commands.
Those who revere You shall see me and rejoice,
because I have hoped in Your word.

I know, Yahweh, that Your decrees are right,
and that You, in faithfulness, have humbled me.
Let Your faithful love be my comfort
according to Your promise to Your servant.

Treat me with tenderness and I shall live,
for Your law is my delight.
Let the arrogant who lie against me be shamed,
while I ponder Your precepts.

Let those who revere You turn to me,
that they may know Your instructions.
May my heart be perfect in Your statutes,
that I may not be ashamed.

All: Glory to Abba our God, to Christ the Word,
and to the Holy Spirit.
As it was in the beginning,
is now and will be for ever. Amen.

Antiphon 2

Those who revere You shall see me and rejoice,
because I have hoped in Your word O God.

Silent Prayer

READING Romans 8:35-39

(*All are seated during the reading.*)

What can separate us from the love of Christ? Can torment, or adversity, or persecution, or famine, or nakedness, or threat, or violence? Even as it is written, "for Your sake we are being killed all the day long; we are counted as sheep to be slaughtered." No, in all these things we are more than conquerors through the One who loves us. For I am certain that neither death nor life, neither angels nor rulers, neither things present nor things to come, neither the heights nor the depths, neither powers nor any other creatures will be able to separate us from the love of God in Christ Jesus our Lord.

(After the reading a period of silence may be observed followed by a brief shared reflection.)

RESPONSORY

Yahweh is true and loves justice.
R. Those who are just will see You face to face.

I know, Yahweh, that Your decrees are right,
R. and the just will see You face to face.

Glory to Abba our God, to Christ the Word,
and to the Holy Spirit.
R. Those who are just will see You face to face.

GOSPEL CANTICLE

(All stand for the Canticle of Mary. Incense may be used during the singing of the Gospel Canticle.)

Antiphon

Treat me with tenderness and I shall live,
for Your law is my delight, O Yahweh.

Song of the Virgin Mary - Luke 1:46-55

My soul proclaims the greatness of Yahweh,
my spirit rejoices in God my Savior;
for Yahweh has looked with favor on this lowly servant,
and henceforth all generations will call me blessed:

"You, the Almighty, have done great things for me,
and Holy is Your Name.
Your compassion is from generation to generation
to those who revere You.

You have brought victory with Your strength
and have dispersed the arrogant of mind and heart.
You have pulled down the mighty from their thrones,
and have raised high the lowly.

You have filled the hungry with good things,
and have dismissed the rich empty handed.

You have come to the help of Israel, Your servant,
remembering Your promise of faithful love,
the promise You made to our ancestors,
to Abraham and to his descendants for ever."

All: Glory to Abba our God, to Christ the Word,
and to the Holy Spirit.
As it was in the beginning,
is now and will be for ever. Amen.

Antiphon

Treat me with tenderness and I shall live,
for Your law is my delight, O Yahweh.

INTERCESSIONS

God is love, and those who live in love, live in God,
and God in them. With love and trust we pray:
R. Guide us by Your Spirit.

Stay with us through out this day, according to Your
promise—and may the light of Your grace never
cease to guide us.
R. Guide us by Your Spirit.

Teach us to pray and to work in Your Church—and
help us to work for the salvation of all people.
R. Guide us by Your Spirit.

Help all Christians to answer Your call to serve—
may they be the salt of the earth and light of the
world.
R. Guide us by Your Spirit.

May the grace of Your Holy Spirit direct our hearts
and our wills—and may we always act in accordance
with Your will.
R. Guide us by Your Spirit.

May those in business and industry work in harmony
for justice—and for the good of the whole community.
R. Guide us by Your Spirit.

(Other prayers may be added.)

THE ABBA PRAYER OF JESUS

CONCLUDING PRAYER

Yahweh God, source of all good,
words cannot measure the boundaries of Your love
for those born to new life in Christ Jesus.
Send Your Spirit to teach us Your truth
and guide our actions in Your way of peace.
Inspire us with good intentions
and help us to put them into practice.
We ask this through Christ our Savior.
R. Amen.

BLESSING

May God bless us, protect us from all evil
and bring us to everlasting life.
R. Amen.

GATHERING PRAYERS 11:
I Hope in Your Word.

INTRODUCTORY VERSE

(*All stand and make the sign of the cross as the leader of prayer says:*)

O God, come to my assistance.
R. Yahweh, make haste to help me.

All: Glory to Abba our God, to Christ the Word,
and to the Holy Spirit.
As it was in the beginning,
is now and will be for ever. Amen.

HYMN

(*An appropriate hymn is sung.*)

PSALMODY

(*During the recitation of the psalms all may sit. Two groups may alternate praying the stanzas of the psalm. The antiphon is prayed by the entire group.*)

Psalm 131 Psalm of Humble Trust in God

Antiphon 1
I have kept my whole being quiet and silent, O Yahweh,
like an infant quieted at its mother's breast.

O Yahweh, my heart is not arrogant,
nor are my eyes raised too high.

I have taken no part in great affairs,
nor in wonders beyond my grasp.

I have kept my whole being quiet and silent,
like an infant quieted at its mother's breast;
like an infant quieted is my whole being.

Let Israel hope in Yahweh
henceforth for all eternity.

All: Glory to Abba our God, to Christ the Word,
and to the Holy Spirit.
As it was in the beginning,
is now and will be for ever. Amen.

Antiphon 1
I have kept my whole being quiet and silent, O Yahweh,
like an infant quieted at its mother's breast.

Silent Prayer

Psalm 119:81-88 God's Law, Our Source of Truth: A Meditative Prayer.

Antiphon 2
Be pleased, O God, to rescue me,
O Yahweh, make haste to help me!

My soul yearns for Your salvation;
I hope in Your word.
My eyes grow bleary awaiting Your promise;
I ask, "When will You comfort me?"

For I have suffered all disgrace,
yet I have not forgotten Your statutes.
How many are the days of Your servant?
When will You bring my persecutors to judgment?

The arrogant have dug a pit for me,
they are not in conformity with Your law.
All Your commands are trustworthy;
help me when they oppress me dishonestly.

They nearly erased me from the earth;
but I did not renounce Your precepts.
In Your faithful love spare my life,
and I will keep the instructions of Your mouth.

All: Glory to Abba our God, to Christ the Word,
and to the Holy Spirit.
As it was in the beginning,
is now and will be for ever. Amen.

Antiphon 2
Be pleased, O God, to rescue me,
O Yahweh, make haste to help me!

Silent Prayer

READING 1 Peter 5:5-7

(*All are seated during the reading.*)

Likewise, you younger ones, show respect to the elder ones, as all of you must show respect to one another. Indeed, all of you should wrap yourselves in the garment of humility toward one another, for God opposes the proud, but gives grace to the humble. Humble yourselves therefore under the mighty hand of God, Who will exalt you in due time. Cast all your anxieties on God, Who cares about you.

(*After the reading a period of silence may be observed followed by a brief shared reflection.*)

RESPONSORY

Cast all your anxieties on God, Who cares about you.
R. Lightly I run the way You have shown.

For my heart is filled with joy,
R. and run the way You have shown.

Glory to Abba our God, to Christ the Word,
and to the Holy Spirit.
R. Lightly I run the way You have shown.

GOSPEL CANTICLE

(All stand for the Canticle of Mary. Incense may be used during the singing of the Gospel Canticle.)

Antiphon

My soul yearns for Your salvation;
I hope in Your word, O Yahweh.

Song of the Virgin Mary - Luke 1:46-55

My soul proclaims the greatness of Yahweh,
my spirit rejoices in God my Savior;
for Yahweh has looked with favor on this lowly servant,
and henceforth all generations will call me blessed:

"You, the Almighty, have done great things for me,
and Holy is Your Name.
Your compassion is from generation to generation
to those who revere You.

You have brought victory with Your strength
and have dispersed the arrogant of mind and heart.
You have pulled down the mighty from their thrones,
and have raised high the lowly.

You have filled the hungry with good things,
and have dismissed the rich empty handed.

You have come to the help of Israel, Your servant,
remembering Your promise of faithful love,
the promise You made to our ancestors,
to Abraham and to his descendants for ever."

All: Glory to Abba our God, to Christ the Word,
and to the Holy Spirit.
As it was in the beginning,
is now and will be for ever. Amen.

Antiphon

My soul yearns for Your salvation;
I hope in Your word, O Yahweh.

INTERCESSIONS

Yahweh, hear our voice when we call to You. You are our help; do not cast us off, do not desert us, our Savior God. With trust we pray:
R. Yahweh God, be with us.

God of our ancestors, remember Your sacred covenant—and fill Your Church with the splendor of Your presence.
R. Yahweh God, be with us.

We thank You for the beauty of creation—and may human hands enhance it for Your greater glory.
R. Yahweh God, be with us.

We are grateful for all the good things we enjoy—teach us to be grateful and to use them well.
R. Yahweh God, be with us.

May we always seek the things that please You—that we may find You in all that we do.
R. Yahweh God, be with us.

To You a thousand years are like a single day—receive those who have died with hope in You.
R. Yahweh God, be with us.

(Other prayers may be added.)

THE ABBA PRAYER OF JESUS

CONCLUDING PRAYER

Almighty and ever-living God,
strength of those who hope in You
sustain us in our prayer.
Give us the grace to follow Christ more closely
and to please You in all that we say and do.
Keep us united in Your constant love,
and help us to live the gospel we profess.
We ask this through Christ our Savior.
R. Amen.

BLESSING

May God bless us, protect us from all evil
and bring us to everlasting life.
R. Amen.

GATHERING PRAYERS 12:

Out of the Depths I Cry to You, Yahweh!

INTRODUCTORY VERSE

(All stand and make the sign of the cross as the leader of prayer says:)

O God, come to my assistance.
R. Yahweh, make haste to help me.

All: Glory to Abba our God, to Christ the Word,
and to the Holy Spirit.
As it was in the beginning,
is now and will be for ever. Amen.

HYMN

(An appropriate hymn is sung.)

PSALMODY

(During the recitation of the psalms all may sit. Two groups may alternate praying the stanzas of the psalm. The antiphon is prayed by the entire group.)

Psalm 130 Prayer for Pardon and Mercy

Antiphon 1

Out of the depths I cry to You, Yahweh!

Out of the depths I cry to You, Yahweh!
Adonai, hear my voice!
Let Your ears be attentive
to my plea for mercy!

If You kept a record of our sins,
Adonai, who could survive?
But with You is forgiveness,
that You may be revered.

I have waited for You, O Yahweh,
my being has waited for Your word.
My whole being waits for Adonai
more than sentinels for daybreak;

more than sentinels for daybreak,
let Israel wait for Yahweh!
For with Yahweh is faithful love,
with Yahweh is abundant redemption.

Yahweh will redeem Israel
from all its sins.

All: Glory to Abba our God, to Christ the Word,
and to the Holy Spirit.
As it was in the beginning,
is now and will be for ever. Amen.

Antiphon 1

Out of the depths I cry to You, Yahweh!

Silent Prayer

Psalm 119:89-96 God's Law, Our Source of Stability: A Meditative Prayer.

Antiphon 2

I will never forget Your precepts, O Yahweh;
for by them You have given me life.

For ever You are, O Yahweh,
Your word is firmly fixed in the heavens.
Your constancy endures to all generations;
You established the earth, and it stands firm.

They continue to abide according to Your decrees,
for all things are Your servants.
Had not Your law been my delight,
I should have perished in my affliction.

I will never forget Your precepts;
for by them You have given me life.
I am Yours, save me;
for I have sought Your precepts.

The wicked lie in wait to destroy me;
but I ponder over Your instructions.
To all perfection I have seen a limit,
but Your Commandments have no limit.

All: Glory to Abba our God, to Christ the Word,
and to the Holy Spirit.
As it was in the beginning,
is now and will be for ever. Amen.

Antiphon 2

I will never forget Your precepts, O Yahweh;
for by them You have given me life.

Silent Prayer

READING Romans 14:12-13,17-19

(All are seated during the reading.)

Every one of us will have to give an account of ourselves before God. Therefore let us not pass judgment on one another, and decide instead never to place an obstacle or put a hindrance in the way of another. It is not eating and drinking that make the Reign of God but the saving justice, the peace and the joy in the Holy Spirit. It is the one who thus serves Christ that will be approved by God and win the esteem of all people. Let us then always seek the ways which lead to peace and the ways in which we can support one another.

(After the reading a period of silence may be observed followed by a brief shared reflection.)

RESPONSORY

Out of the depths I cry to You, Yahweh!
R. Support me, Yahweh, and I shall live.

Let my hope in You be not in vain,
R. and I shall live.

Glory to Abba our God, to Christ the Word,
and to the Holy Spirit.
R. Support me, Yahweh, and I shall live.

GOSPEL CANTICLE

(All stand for the Canticle of Mary. Incense may be used during the singing of the Gospel Canticle.)

Antiphon

For ever You are, O Yahweh,
Your word is firmly fixed in the heavens.

Song of the Virgin Mary - Luke 1:46-55

My soul proclaims the greatness of Yahweh,
my spirit rejoices in God my Savior;
for Yahweh has looked with favor on this lowly servant,
and henceforth all generations will call me blessed:

"You, the Almighty, have done great things for me,
and Holy is Your Name.
Your compassion is from generation to generation
to those who revere You.

You have brought victory with Your strength
and have dispersed the arrogant of mind and heart.
You have pulled down the mighty from their thrones,
and have raised high the lowly.

You have filled the hungry with good things,
and have dismissed the rich empty handed.

You have come to the help of Israel, Your servant,
remembering Your promise of faithful love,
the promise You made to our ancestors,
to Abraham and to his descendants for ever."

All: Glory to Abba our God, to Christ the Word,
and to the Holy Spirit.
As it was in the beginning,
is now and will be for ever. Amen.

Antiphon

For ever You are, O Yahweh,
Your word is firmly fixed in the heavens.

INTERCESSIONS

Let us pray to Yahweh our Good Shepherd, who loves us with the love of both a father and a mother and always hears our prayers:
R. May we grow in love, O God.

We thank You for enlightening us through Christ, the true light—may we keep Christ before our eyes throughout our lives.
R. May we grow in love, O God.

Give us new life at the table of the Word and the Eucharist—strengthened by this food may we follow You with joy.
R. May we grow in love, O God.

Give us strength in our weakness for Your name's sake—and enable us to serve You with greater generosity.
R. May we grow in love, O God.

You have shown the sick and the suffering Your compassionate love—give them strength and patience in their pain.
R. May we grow in love, O God.

Welcome all who have died in Your Peace—bring them to everlasting life with all Your holy ones.
R. May we grow in love, O God.

(Other prayers may be added.)

THE ABBA PRAYER OF JESUS

CONCLUDING PRAYER

Ever-loving God,
our hope and our strength,
we rejoice to call You Abba, our God.
Protect us with Your guiding hand,
grant us an unfailing respect for Your name,
and keep us one in Your peace, secure in Your love.
Open the gates of heaven to those who have died,
and be their shepherd for ever.
We ask this through Christ our Savior.
R. Amen.

BLESSING

May God bless us, protect us from all evil
and bring us to everlasting life.
R. Amen.

GATHERING PRAYERS 13:

Be at Peace with Everyone.

INTRODUCTORY VERSE

(*All stand and make the sign of the cross as the leader of prayer says:*)

O God, come to my assistance.
R. Yahweh, make haste to help me.

All: Glory to Abba our God, to Christ the Word,
and to the Holy Spirit.
As it was in the beginning,
is now and will be for ever. Amen.

HYMN

(*An appropriate hymn is sung.*)

PSALMODY

(*During the recitation of the psalms all may sit. Two groups may alternate praying the stanzas of the psalm. The antiphon is prayed by the entire group.*)

Psalm 133 True Communion of God's People

Antiphon 1

Praise, O servants of Yahweh,
Praise the name of Yahweh!

How very good, how delightful it is
when kindred live together in unity!

It is like the precious oil on the head,
running down upon the beard,
running down upon Aaron's beard,
onto the collar of his robes!

It is like the dew of Hermon,
falling on the mountains of Zion.
For there Yahweh bestows the blessing,
life for evermore!

All: Glory to Abba our God, to Christ the Word,
and to the Holy Spirit.
As it was in the beginning,
is now and will be for ever. Amen.

Antiphon 1

Praise, O servants of Yahweh,
Praise the name of Yahweh!

Silent Prayer

Psalm 119:97-104 God's Law, Our Source of Wisdom: A Meditative Prayer.

Antiphon 2

How pleasant is Your promise to my palate,
yes, sweeter than honey to my mouth!

Oh, how I love Your law!
I meditate on it all day long.
Your Command makes me wiser than my foes,
because it is ever with me.

I have more wisdom than all my teachers,
for Your instructions are my meditation.
I have more insight than the elders,
for I keep Your precepts.

I have kept my feet from every evil path,
in order to keep Your word.
I have not departed from Your decrees,
since You Yourself have taught me.

How pleasant is Your promise to my palate,
yes, sweeter than honey to my mouth!
From Your precepts I gain insight;
so I hate all deceptive ways.

All: Glory to Abba our God, to Christ the Word,
and to the Holy Spirit.
As it was in the beginning,
is now and will be for ever. Amen.

Antiphon 2

How pleasant is Your promise to my palate,
yes, sweeter than honey to my mouth!

Silent Prayer

READING Romans 12:13-18

(*All are seated during the reading.*)

Share with God's holy people who are in need. Look for opportunities to be hospitable. Bless those who mistreat you, never curse them, bless them instead. Rejoice with those who rejoice, mourn with those who mourn. Care as much about others as about yourselves; do not pay attention to the social standing; associate with the humble people. Do not claim to be wiser than you are. Do not repay anyone evil for evil. Bear in mind the ideals that all regard with respect. As much as possible, and to the utmost of your ability, be at peace with every one.

(*After the reading a period of silence may be observed followed by a brief shared reflection.*)

RESPONSORY

The decrees of Yahweh are true, all of them just.
R. The reverence of Yahweh is holy, enduring for ever.

The precepts of Yahweh are sweeter than honey,
R. enduring for ever.

Glory to Abba our God, to Christ the Word,
and to the Holy Spirit.
R. The reverence of Yahweh is holy, enduring for ever.

GOSPEL CANTICLE

(*All stand for the Canticle of Mary. Incense may be used during the singing of the Gospel Canticle.*)

Antiphon

Your compassion is from generation to generation
to those who revere You, O Yahweh.

Song of the Virgin Mary - Luke 1:46-55

My soul proclaims the greatness of Yahweh,
my spirit rejoices in God my Savior;
for Yahweh has looked with favor on this lowly servant,
and henceforth all generations will call me blessed:

"You, the Almighty, have done great things for me,
and Holy is Your Name.
Your compassion is from generation to generation
to those who revere You.

You have brought victory with Your strength
and have dispersed the arrogant of mind and heart.
You have pulled down the mighty from their thrones,
and have raised high the lowly.

You have filled the hungry with good things,
and have dismissed the rich empty handed.

You have come to the help of Israel, Yours
remembering Your promise of faithful love,
the promise You made to our ancestors,
to Abraham and to his descendants for ever."

All: Glory to Abba our God, to Christ the Word,
and to the Holy Spirit.
As it was in the beginning,
is now and will be for ever. Amen.

Antiphon

Your compassion is from generation to generation
to those who revere You, O Yahweh.

INTERCESSIONS

Jesus prayed, "Abba, I pray for them: may they be one in us, so that the world may believe it was You who sent me." Let us invoke Christ as we pray for unity:
R. May we be united in Your Love.

We celebrate Your kindness and compassion Christ Jesus—may we be united with all through love and understanding.
R. May we be united in Your Love.

In recalling Your death and resurrection—may we receive the fruits of Your redemption.
R. May we be united in Your Love.

Grant that we may bear witness to You this day—and offer an acceptable gift to Abba, our God, through You.
R. May we be united in Your Love.

Enable us to see You in all people—and serve You in all especially in the poor and the oppressed.
R. May we be united in Your Love.

You are the true vine and we are the branches—may we remain united in You to bear fruit and give glory to Abba our God.
R. May we be united in Your Love.

(*Other prayers may be added.*)

THE ABBA PRAYER OF JESUS

CONCLUDING PRAYER

God in heaven,
You have made us children of light,
who walk in the light of Christ.
Keep us always in the radiance of Your truth.
and give us the strength to reject what is evil.
Grant that Your light may shine within us,
and form our lives in Your truth,
our hearts in Your love.
We ask this through Christ our Savior.
R. Amen.

BLESSING

May God bless us, protect us from all evil
and bring us to everlasting life.
R. Amen.

GATHERING PRAYERS 14:

My Life Is in Your Hands Forever.

INTRODUCTORY VERSE

(All stand and make the sign of the cross as the leader of prayer says:)

O God, come to my assistance.
R. Yahweh, make haste to help me.

All: Glory to Abba our God, to Christ the Word,
and to the Holy Spirit.
As it was in the beginning,
is now and will be for ever. Amen.

HYMN

(An appropriate hymn is sung.)

PSALMODY

(During the recitation of the psalms all may sit. Two groups may alternate praying the stanzas of the psalm. The antiphon is prayed by the entire group.)

Psalm 27:7-14 A Prayer in Time of Affliction

Antiphon 1

Though my father and my mother forsake me,
You, Yahweh, will uphold me.

Hear, O Yahweh, the sound of my call,
have mercy on me and answer me!
My heart says to You, "Seek my face."
"Your face, Yahweh, do I seek."

Do not hide Your face from me;
do not turn Your servant away in anger.
You are my help, do not leave me
do not forsake me, O God my Savior!

Though my father and my mother forsake me,
You, Yahweh, will uphold me.
Yahweh, teach me Your way,
and lead me on the path of justice.

Because of those who watch me,
do not deliver me into the hands of my enemies;
for false witnesses have risen against me,
and are breathing out violence.

I believe that I shall see
the goodness of Yahweh in the land of the living!
Trust in Yahweh, and be of good courage;
let your heart take courage, yes, trust in Yahweh!

All: Glory to Abba our God, to Christ the Word,
and to the Holy Spirit.

As it was in the beginning,
is now and will be for ever. Amen.

Antiphon 1

Though my father and my mother forsake me,
You, Yahweh, will uphold me.

Silent Prayer

Psalm 119:105-112 God's Law, Our Light on Our Path: A Meditative Prayer.

Antiphon 2

Accept, Yahweh, my offerings of praise,
and teach me Your decrees.

Your word is a lamp for my feet
a light on my path.
I have sworn and will persevere
in observing Your just decrees.

I am sorely afflicted, O Yahweh;
give me life according to Your word!
Accept, Yahweh, my offerings of praise,
and teach me Your decrees.

My life is in Your hands for ever,
let me not forget Your law.
The wicked have laid a snare for me,
but I have not strayed from Your precepts.

Your instructions are my eternal heritage,
they are the joy of my heart.
I devote myself to obeying Your statutes,
their recompense is eternal.

All: Glory to Abba our God, to Christ the Word,
and to the Holy Spirit.
As it was in the beginning,
is now and will be for ever. Amen.

Antiphon 2

Accept, Yahweh, my offerings of praise,
and teach me Your decrees.

Silent Prayer

READING James 2:12-17

(*All are seated during the reading.*)

Always speak and act as people who will be judged by the law of freedom. Whoever acts mercilessly will be judged without mercy. Mercy rejoices over judgment.

What good is it, my brothers and sisters, if you say you have faith but do not have a single good deed? Can faith save you? If a brother or sister has nothing to wear and has no food for the day, and you were to say to them, "I wish you well; keep yourselves warm, and eat plenty," without giving them these bare necessities of life, what good is that? So faith by itself, if it has no good deeds, is dead.

(*After the reading a period of silence may be observed followed by a brief shared reflection.*)

RESPONSORY

Your instructions are my eternal heritage.
R. Yahweh, our God, You are the well-spring of life.

Accept, Yahweh, my offerings of praise,
R. You are the well-spring of life.

Glory to Abba our God, to Christ the Word,
and to the Holy Spirit.
R. Yahweh, our God, You are the well-spring of life.

GOSPEL CANTICLE

(*All stand for the Canticle of Mary. Incense may be used during the singing of the Gospel Canticle.*)

Antiphon
Yahweh, our God, You are the well-spring of life.

Song of the Virgin Mary - Luke 1:46-55
My soul proclaims the greatness of Yahweh,
my spirit rejoices in God my Savior;
for Yahweh has looked with favor on this lowly servant,
and henceforth all generations will call me blessed:

"You, the Almighty, have done great things for me,
and Holy is Your Name.
Your compassion is from generation to generation
to those who revere You.

You have brought victory with Your strength
and have dispersed the arrogant of mind and heart.
You have pulled down the mighty from their thrones,
and have raised high the lowly.

You have filled the hungry with good things,
and have dismissed the rich empty handed.

You have come to the help of Israel, Your servant,
remembering Your promise of faithful love,
the promise You made to our ancestors,
to Abraham and to his descendants for ever."

All: Glory to Abba our God, to Christ the Word,
and to the Holy Spirit.
As it was in the beginning,
is now and will be for ever. Amen.

Antiphon
Yahweh, our God, You are the well-spring of life.

INTERCESSIONS

Jesus says: "Come to me, all you that labor and are burdened, and I will give you rest." Let us place our trust in God's providence as we pray:
R. Abba, our God, we trust in You.

We bless You, Abba, our God, for bringing us to this day—we thank You for protecting our lives and giving us what we need.
R. Abba, our God, we trust in You.

Be with us as we take up our daily tasks—help us to remember that the world we live and work is Yours.
R. Abba, our God, we trust in You.

God, redeemer and creator of humankind, we humbly pray for people of every race and nation,—make Your ways known to them and reveal Your salvation to all nations.
R. Abba, our God, we trust in You.

Stay with us and with everyone we meet this day—help us to spread Your joy and peace to all in the world.
R. Abba, our God, we trust in You.

(*Other prayers may be added.*)

THE ABBA PRAYER OF JESUS

CONCLUDING PRAYER

God in heaven,
in the sufferings, death and rising of Jesus,
You raised a fallen world.
Give us grace to rejoice in the freedom from sin
and bring us the joy that lasts for ever.
Grant us greater willingness
to serve You in our brothers and sisters.
We ask this through Christ our Savior.
R. Amen.

BLESSING

May God bless us, protect us from all evil
and bring us to everlasting life.
R. Amen.

GATHERING PRAYERS 15:

You Are My Protector and My Shield.

INTRODUCTORY VERSE

(All stand and make the sign of the cross as the leader of prayer says:)

O God, come to my assistance.
R. Yahweh, make haste to help me.

All: Glory to Abba our God, to Christ the Word,
and to the Holy Spirit.
As it was in the beginning,
is now and will be for ever. Amen.

HYMN

(An appropriate hymn is sung.)

PSALMODY

(During the recitation of the psalms all may sit. Two groups may alternate praying the stanzas of the psalm. The antiphon is prayed by the entire group.)

Psalm 128 Rewards of those Trust in God

Antiphon 1
May Yahweh bless us from Zion!

Blessed are those who revere Yahweh,
and those who walk in God's ways!
You shall eat the fruit of your handiwork;
you shall be happy and prosperous.

Your spouse will be like a fruitful vine
by the sides of your house;
your children will be like olive plants
around your table.

Behold, thus one is blessed,
who reveres Yahweh.
May Yahweh bless you from Zion!

May you see the prosperity of Jerusalem
all the days of your life!
May you see your children's children!
Peace be upon Israel!

All: Glory to Abba our God, to Christ the Word,
and to the Holy Spirit.
As it was in the beginning,
is now and will be for ever. Amen.

Antiphon 1
May Yahweh bless us from Zion!

Silent Prayer

Psalm 119:113-120 God's Law, Our Source of Protection: A Meditative Prayer.

Antiphon 2
You are my Protector and my shield;
I hope in Your word, O Yahweh.

I hate a divided heart,
but I love Your law.
You are my Protector and my shield;
I hope in Your word.

Depart from me, you wicked,
that I may observe the commands of my God.
True to Your promise, sustain me and I shall live,
do not let me be ashamed in my hope.

Uphold me and I shall be saved,
that I may always respect Your statutes.
You reject all who go astray from Your statutes;
for they worship falsehood.

You reject as dross all the wicked of the earth,
so I love Your instructions.
My whole body trembles before You,
Your decrees fill me with awe.

All: Glory to Abba our God, to Christ the Word,
and to the Holy Spirit.
As it was in the beginning,
is now and will be for ever. Amen.

Antiphon 2
You are my Protector and my shield;
I hope in Your word, O Yahweh.

Silent Prayer

READING James 4:11-12

(All are seated during the reading.)

Brothers and sisters, do not speak evil against one another. Whoever speaks evil against another or passes judgment on another, speaks against the law and condemns the law. If you condemn the law, you are not keeping it but become a judge over it. There is only one lawgiver and judge, the One Who has the power to save and to destroy. So who are you to pass judgment on your neighbor?

(After the reading a period of silence may be observed followed by a brief shared reflection.)

RESPONSORY

True to Your promise, sustain me and I shall live.
R. O Yahweh, I cried to You for help.

And You, my God, have healed me,
R. I cried to You for help.

Glory to Abba our God, to Christ the Word,
and to the Holy Spirit.
R. O Yahweh, I cried to You for help.

GOSPEL CANTICLE

(All stand for the Canticle of Mary. Incense may be used during the singing of the Gospel Canticle.)

Antiphon

Uphold me and I shall be saved, O God,
that I may always respect Your statutes.

Song of the Virgin Mary - Luke 1:46-55

My soul proclaims the greatness of Yahweh,
my spirit rejoices in God my Savior;
for Yahweh has looked with favor on this lowly servant,
and henceforth all generations will call me blessed:

"You, the Almighty, have done great things for me,
and Holy is Your Name.
Your compassion is from generation to generation
to those who revere You.

You have brought victory with Your strength
and have dispersed the arrogant of mind and heart.
You have pulled down the mighty from their thrones,
and have raised high the lowly.

You have filled the hungry with good things,
and have dismissed the rich empty handed.

You have come to the help of Israel, Your servant,
remembering Your promise of faithful love,
the promise You made to our ancestors,
to Abraham and to his descendants for ever."

All: Glory to Abba our God, to Christ the Word,
and to the Holy Spirit.
As it was in the beginning,
is now and will be for ever. Amen.

Antiphon

Uphold me and I shall be saved, O God,
that I may always respect Your statutes.

INTERCESSIONS

Jesus said: "Those who eat my flesh and drink my blood will live in me and I in them." Let us implore Christ our Savior and pray:
R. May we find peace in You.

Blessed are You, Christ our Savior, for You have redeemed us by Your precious blood—and grant us the glorious liberty of the children of God.
R. May we find peace in You.

Endow with plentiful grace all those who hold pastoral leadership—grant them courage and compassion in their ministry.
R. May we find peace in You.

Grant to all who explore truth may find what they seek—may they be consecrated in truth.
R. May we find peace in You.

Keep orphans, widows, homeless, and all the destitute in the shelter of Your love—comfort them and be with them in their need.
R. May we find peace in You.

Mercifully receive those who have died into the heavenly city—where You will be all in all and their joy will be full.
R. May we find peace in You.

(Other prayers may be added.)

THE ABBA PRAYER OF JESUS

CONCLUDING PRAYER

God our Creator,
let the light of Your truth
guide us to the way of Christ.
Grant that all who have received baptism
may strive to be worthy of their calling
and reject what is contrary to the gospel.
Help us to follow the light of faith,
and to make Your gospel our rule of life.
We ask this through Christ our Savior.
R. Amen.

BLESSING

May God bless us, protect us from all evil
and bring us to everlasting life.
R. Amen.

GATHERING PRAYERS 16:
Give Me Understanding, O God!

INTRODUCTORY VERSE

(*All stand and make the sign of the cross as the leader of prayer says*:)

O God, come to my assistance.
R. Yahweh, make haste to help me.

All: Glory to Abba our God, to Christ the Word,
and to the Holy Spirit.
As it was in the beginning,
is now and will be for ever. Amen.

HYMN

(*An appropriate hymn is sung.*)

PSALMODY

(*During the recitation of the psalms all may sit. Two groups may alternate praying the stanzas of the psalm. The antiphon is prayed by the entire group.*)

Psalm 47:1-8 A Hymn to Yahweh, the Sovereign of Nations

Antiphon 1

Sing praise to God, sing praise!
Sing praise to our Ruler, sing praise!

Clap your hands, all you peoples!
Shout aloud to God with songs of joy!
For Yahweh, the Most High, the Awesome,
is a great ruler over all the earth.

Yahweh humbled peoples in our sight,
and subdued the nations.
Yahweh has chosen our inheritance for us:
the glory of beloved Israel.

God mounts the throne amid shouts of joy,
Yahweh with the sound of a trumpet.
Sing praise to God, sing praise!
Sing praise to our Ruler, sing praise!

For God is the ruler of all the earth;
sing a psalm for edification.
God reigns over the nations;
God sits on the throne of Holiness.

All: Glory to Abba our God, to Christ the Word,
and to the Holy Spirit.
As it was in the beginning,
is now and will be for ever. Amen.

Antiphon 1

Sing praise to God, sing praise!
Sing praise to our Ruler, sing praise!

Silent Prayer

Psalm 119:121-128 God's Law, Our Source of Freedom: A Meditative Prayer.

Antiphon 2

Give me understanding, O God,
that I may know Your instructions.

I have practiced Your just decrees;
do not hand me over to my oppressors.
Assure the well-being of Your servant;
do not let the arrogant oppress me.

My eyes are languishing for Your salvation,
and for the promise of Your saving justice.
Deal with me according to Your faithful love,
and teach Your servant Your statutes.

Give me understanding, I am Your servant;
that I may know Your instructions.
It is time to take action, Yahweh,
for Your law is being broken.

So I love Your commands
more than gold, purest gold.
So I consider right all Your precepts,
I hate all ways of falsehood.

All: Glory to Abba our God, to Christ the Word,
and to the Holy Spirit
As it was in the beginning,
is now and will be for ever. Amen.

Antiphon 2

Give me understanding, O God,
that I may know Your instructions.

Silent Prayer

READING 1 John 4:12-15

(*All are seated during the reading.*)

No one has ever seen God. If we love one another, God lives in us and God's love is perfected in us. This is how we know that we live in God and God in us, because of the Divine Spirit given to us. As for us, we have seen and can testify that Abba our God has sent the Only-begotten as the Savior of the world. God lives in those who acknowledge that Jesus is the Only-begotten of God, and they live in God.

(After the reading a period of silence may be observed followed by a brief shared reflection.)

RESPONSORY

Yahweh will render all people their just reward.
R. For God is the ruler of all the earth.

Yahweh will judge the whole world with justice,
R. the ruler of all the earth.

Glory to Abba our God, to Christ the Word,
and to the Holy Spirit.
R. For God is the ruler of all the earth.

GOSPEL CANTICLE

(All stand for the Canticle of Mary. Incense may be used during the singing of the Gospel Canticle.)

Antiphon

Yahweh will render all people their just reward.

Song of the Virgin Mary - Luke 1:46-55

My soul proclaims the greatness of Yahweh,
my spirit rejoices in God my Savior;
for Yahweh has looked with favor on this lowly servant,
and henceforth all generations will call me blessed:

"You, the Almighty, have done great things for me,
and Holy is Your Name.
Your compassion is from generation to generation
to those who revere You.
You have brought victory with Your strength
and have dispersed the arrogant of mind and heart.
You have pulled down the mighty from their thrones,
and have raised high the lowly.

You have filled the hungry with good things,
and have dismissed the rich empty handed.

You have come to the help of Israel, Your servant,
remembering Your promise of faithful love,
the promise You made to our ancestors,
to Abraham and to his descendants for ever."

All: Glory to Abba our God, to Christ the Word,
and to the Holy Spirit.
As it was in the beginning,
is now and will be for ever. Amen.

Antiphon

Yahweh will render all people their just reward.

INTERCESSIONS

Yahweh, our God, is gracious and merciful. Let us place all our hope in God, the shepherd and guardian of our souls as we pray:
R. Be merciful to us, O eternal Shepherd.

You are our hope and our courage, look with mercy on those who suffer persecution—and sustain them in their pain and isolation.
R. Be merciful to us, O eternal Shepherd.

You are our joy and solace—remember the poor and afflicted that this day may not be a burden to them.
R. Be merciful to us, O eternal Shepherd.

You are our eternal shepherd, bring healing to the sick and give bread to the hungry—comfort and sustain all who are in want.
R. Be merciful to us, O eternal Shepherd.

You are our sovereign ruler, enlighten those who are appointed to the work of legislation—that they may enact laws in the spirit of wisdom and justice.
R. Be merciful to us, O eternal Shepherd.

You are our merciful judge, come to the aid of Your faithful departed, redeemed by the precious blood of Christ—may they be found worthy to praise and bless You for ever in heaven.
R. Be merciful to us, O eternal Shepherd.

(Other prayers may be added.)

THE ABBA PRAYER OF JESUS

CONCLUDING PRAYER

God of ever-lasting goodness,
be merciful to us who serve You
and in Your kindness let the gift of Your life
continue to grow in us,
drawing us from death to faith, hope, and love.
Keep us watchful in prayer
and faithful to Christ's teaching
till Your glory is revealed in us.
We ask this through Christ our Savior.
R. Amen.

BLESSING

May God bless us, protect us from all evil
and bring us to everlasting life.
R. Amen.

GATHERING PRAYERS 17:
Yahweh Will Guard You from All Evil.

INTRODUCTORY VERSE

(All stand and make the sign of the cross as the leader of prayer says:)

O God, come to my assistance.
R. Yahweh, make haste to help me.

All: Glory to Abba our God, to Christ the Word,
and to the Holy Spirit.
As it was in the beginning,
is now and will be for ever. Amen.

HYMN

(An appropriate hymn is sung.)

PSALMODY

(During the recitation of the psalms all may sit. Two groups may alternate praying the stanzas of the psalm. The antiphon is prayed by the entire group.)

Psalm 121 Yahweh, the Guardian of Israel

Antiphon 1

Yahweh will guard you from all evil.

I raise my eyes to the Mountain,
whence will help come to me?
My help comes from Yahweh,
who made heaven and earth.

Yahweh will not let your foot to slip,
Yahweh, your guardian will not slumber.
Behold, the guardian of Israel
shall neither sleep nor slumber.

Yahweh is your guardian;
Yahweh is your shade on your right hand.
The sun shall not scourge you by day,
nor shall the moon by night.

Yahweh will guard you from all evil;
Yahweh will guard your life.
Yahweh will guard your goings and coming
henceforth unto eternity.

All: Glory to Abba our God, to Christ the Word,
and to the Holy Spirit.
As it was in the beginning,
is now and will be for ever. Amen.

Antiphon 1

Yahweh will guard you from all evil.

Silent Prayer

Psalm 119:129-136 God's Law, Our Source of Light: A Meditative Prayer.

Antiphon 2

Turn to me and be gracious to me, O Yahweh,
as is Your Decree to those who love Your Name.

Your instructions are wonderful;
so my soul observes them.
The unfolding of Your word gives light;
it imparts insight to the simple.

With gasping mouth I panted,
in my yearning for Your commands.
Turn to me and be gracious to me,
as is Your Decree to those who love Your Name.

Steady my steps according to Your promise,
let not wickedness triumph over me.
Rescue me from human oppression,
that I may observe Your precepts.

Make Your face shine upon Your servant,
and teach me Your statutes.
My eyes shed streams of tears,
because Your law is not observed.

All: Glory to Abba our God, to Christ the Word,
and to the Holy Spirit.
As it was in the beginning,
is now and will be for ever. Amen.

Antiphon 2

Turn to me and be gracious to me, O Yahweh,
as is Your Decree to those who love Your Name.

Silent Prayer

READING Romans 12:9-12

(All are seated during the reading.)

Let love be genuine. Avoid what is evil and hold on to what is good. Love one another with mutual affection. Outdo one another in showing esteem. Do not grow slack in zeal, be ardent in spirit, serve Yahweh. Rejoice in hope, be patient in suffering, and persevere in prayer.

(After the reading a period of silence may be observed followed by a brief shared reflection.)

RESPONSORY

All who seek You, Yahweh, will dance for joy.
R. They will proclaim Your greatness for ever.

Steady my steps according to Your promise,
R. and I will proclaim Your greatness for ever.

Glory to Abba our God, to Christ the Word,
and to the Holy Spirit.
R. They will proclaim Your greatness for ever.

GOSPEL CANTICLE

(*All stand for the Canticle of Mary. Incense may be used during the singing of the Gospel Canticle.*)

Antiphon

The unfolding of Your Word gives light;
it imparts insight to the simple, O Yahweh.

Song of the Virgin Mary - Luke 1:46-55

My soul proclaims the greatness of Yahweh,
my spirit rejoices in God my Savior;
for Yahweh has looked with favor on this lowly servant,
and henceforth all generations will call me blessed:

"You, the Almighty, have done great things for me,
and Holy is Your Name.
Your compassion is from generation to generation
to those who revere You.

You have brought victory with Your strength
and have dispersed the arrogant of mind and heart.
You have pulled down the mighty from their thrones,
and have raised high the lowly.

You have filled the hungry with good things,
and have dismissed the rich empty handed.

You have come to the help of Israel, Your servant,
remembering Your promise of faithful love,
the promise You made to our ancestors,
to Abraham and to his descendants for ever."

All: Glory to Abba our God, to Christ the Word,
and to the Holy Spirit.
As it was in the beginning,
is now and will be for ever. Amen.

Antiphon

The unfolding of Your word gives light;
it imparts insight to the simple, O Yahweh.

INTERCESSIONS

Happy are those who show mercy; mercy shall be theirs. Nothing can break the confidence of those whom God has established in hope. With trust we pray:
R. Abba our God, our trust is in You.

We thank You O God, for You have remade us in Christ Jesus—with the word of truth and with understanding.
R. Abba our God, our trust is in You.

Give Your wisdom to those who govern our country and all nations—may they work for the good of all people they govern.
R. Abba our God, our trust is in You.

It is by Your gift that artists are able to express Your beauty—use their work to brighten our world with hope and joy.
R. Abba our God, our trust is in You.

You never allow us to be tested beyond our ability—strengthen the weak and raise up those who have fallen.
R. Abba our God, our trust is in You.

You have promised that the dead will be raised to life—be ever mindful of those who have gone before us on the path to eternal life.
R. Abba our God, our trust is in You.

(*Other prayers may be added.*)

THE ABBA PRAYER OF JESUS

CONCLUDING PRAYER

Yahweh God, our creator,
protector of those who hope in You,
without You nothing is strong, nothing holy.
Help us to recognize Your presence in our world
and to make good use of the gifts You have given us.
Help us to cherish the gifts that surround us,
to share Your blessings with our brothers and sisters,
and to experience the joy of life in Your presence.
We ask this through Christ our Savior.
R. Amen.

BLESSING

May God bless us, protect us from all evil
and bring us to everlasting life.
R. Amen.

GATHERING PRAYERS 18:
Let Us Go to the House of Yahweh!

INTRODUCTORY VERSE

(*All stand and make the sign of the cross as the leader of prayer says:*)

O God, come to my assistance.
R. Yahweh, make haste to help me.

All: Glory to Abba our God, to Christ the Word,
and to the Holy Spirit.
As it was in the beginning,
is now and will be for ever. Amen.

HYMN

(*An appropriate hymn is sung.*)

PSALMODY

(*During the recitation of the psalms all may sit. Two groups may alternate praying the stanzas of the psalm. The antiphon is prayed by the entire group.*)

Psalm 122 Pilgrim's Blessings on the Holy City

Antiphon 1

Let there be peace within your walls.

I rejoiced when I heard them say,
"Let us go to the house of Yahweh!"
At last we have set foot,
within your gates, O Jerusalem!

Jerusalem, built as a city
which is bound firmly together,
There the tribes go up,
the tribes of Yahweh.

It is a decree for Israel
to give thanks to the Name of Yahweh.
In it are established thrones of justice,
the thrones of the house of David.

"May they pray for your peace, Jerusalem!
May they prosper who love you!
Let there be peace within your walls,
and prosperity within your dwellings!"

For the sake of my relatives and companions,
I will say, "Peace be within you!"
For the sake of the house of Yahweh our God,
I will pray for your well-being.

All: Glory to Abba our God, to Christ the Word,
and to the Holy Spirit.
As it was in the beginning,
is now and will be for ever. Amen.

Antiphon 1

Let there be peace within your walls.

Silent Prayer

Psalm 119:137-144 God's Law, Our Source of Delight: A Meditative Prayer.

Antiphon 2

Your justice is eternally just, O God.

O Yahweh, You are just,
Your decrees are fitting.
You have established Your instructions
in justice and perfect faithfulness.

My zeal is burning me up,
because my enemies ignore Your word.
Your promise is well tested
and Your servant holds it dear.

I am insignificant and abject,
yet I do not forget Your precepts.
Your justice is eternally just,
and Your law is trustworthy.

Distress and anguish have come upon me,
but Your commands are my delight.
Your instructions are eternally just,
give me insight that I may live.

All: Glory to Abba our God, to Christ the Word,
and to the Holy Spirit.
As it was in the beginning,
is now and will be for ever. Amen.

Antiphon 2

Your justice is eternally just, O God.

Silent Prayer

READING Ephesians 3:17-21

(*All are seated during the reading.*)

I pray that Christ may dwell in your hearts through faith as you are being rooted and grounded in love. I pray that you may have the strength to comprehend with all God's holy people, what is the breadth and the length, the height and the depth of the love of Christ which is beyond knowledge. May you attain the fullness of being, the very fullness of God.

Glory be to the One whose power, working in us, can do infinitely more than we can ask or imagine. Glory be to the One from generation to generation in the Church and in Christ Jesus for ever and ever. Amen.

(After the reading a period of silence may be observed followed by a brief shared reflection.)

RESPONSORY

Your justice, O God, is eternally just.
R. Your instructions are eternally just.

You have established Your instructions,
R. eternally just.

Glory to Abba our God, to Christ the Word,
and to the Holy Spirit.
R. Your instructions are eternally just.

GOSPEL CANTICLE

(All stand for the Canticle of Mary. Incense may be used during the singing of the Gospel Canticle.)

Antiphon

"God, the Almighty, has done great things for me.

Song of the Virgin Mary - Luke 1:46-55

My soul proclaims the greatness of Yahweh,
my spirit rejoices in God my Savior;
for Yahweh has looked with favor on this lowly servant,
and henceforth all generations will call me blessed:

"You, the Almighty, have done great things for me,
and Holy is Your Name.
Your compassion is from generation to generation
to those who revere You.

You have brought victory with Your strength
and have dispersed the arrogant of mind and heart.
You have pulled down the mighty from their thrones,
and have raised high the lowly.

You have filled the hungry with good things,
and have dismissed the rich empty handed.

You have come to the help of Israel, Your servant,
remembering Your promise of faithful love,
the promise You made to our ancestors,
to Abraham and to his descendants for ever."

All: Glory to Abba our God, to Christ the Word,
and to the Holy Spirit.
As it was in the beginning,
is now and will be for ever. Amen.

Antiphon

God, the Almighty, has done great things for me.

INTERCESSIONS

We may have faith strong enough to move mountains, but if we have no love, we are nothing. We ask God to fill us with love as we pray:
R. Grant us Your love, O God.

We thank You, O God, for You have chosen us as Your people for all eternity—and have called us to receive the glory of Christ our Savior.
R. Grant us Your love, O God.

When assailed by doubts and weighed down by uncertainties—release our hearts to journey towards You with hope.
R. Grant us Your love, O God.

Confirm the pilgrim Church in the faith of the Apostles—help us to encourage each other, sharing our gifts.
R. Grant us Your love, O God.

We pray for Christians who suffer for their belief—sustain them in their hope.
R. Grant us Your love, O God.

Bring those who have died in Your peace—grant them the fullness of Your love.
R. Grant us Your love, O God.

(Other prayers may be added.)

THE ABBA PRAYER OF JESUS

CONCLUDING PRAYER

God of everlasting goodness,
You are our origin and source of life,
and Your kindness never fails.
Guide our life's journey,
by Your providence and unfailing love.
Renew Your life within us
and keep us strong in Your peace and love,
for gifts without measure flow from your goodness.
We ask this through Christ our Savior.
R. Amen.

BLESSING

May God bless us, protect us from all evil
and bring us to everlasting life.
R. Amen.

GATHERING PRAYERS 19:

Be Gracious to Us, O Yahweh.

INTRODUCTORY VERSE

(All stand and make the sign of the cross as the leader of prayer says:)

O God, come to my assistance.
R. Yahweh, make haste to help me.

All: Glory to Abba our God, to Christ the Word,
and to the Holy Spirit.
As it was in the beginning,
is now and will be for ever. Amen.

HYMN

(An appropriate hymn is sung.)

PSALMODY

(During the recitation of the psalms all may sit. Two groups may alternate praying the stanzas of the psalm. The antiphon is prayed by the entire group.)

Psalm 123 Collective Entreaty for God's Mercy

Antiphon 1

Be gracious to us, O Yahweh, be gracious to us.

I raise my eyes to You,
Who are enthroned in heaven!
Like the eyes of a servant
are on the hand of his master,

Like the eyes of a servant
are on the hand of her mistress,
so our eyes are on You, Yahweh our God
till You are gracious to us.

Be gracious to us, O Yahweh,
be gracious to us,
for we have been sated with contempt.

Our souls are more than sated
with the mockery of the arrogant,
with the contempt of the haughty.

All: Glory to Abba our God, to Christ the Word,
and to the Holy Spirit.
As it was in the beginning,
is now and will be for ever. Amen.

Antiphon 1

Be gracious to us, O Yahweh, be gracious to us.

Silent Prayer

Psalm 119:145-152 God's Law, Our Source of Faithfulness: A Meditative Prayer.

Antiphon 2

In Your faithful love, Yahweh, listen to my voice,
let Your decrees give me life.

I call with all my heart, Yahweh, answer me,
and I will observe Your statutes.
I call to You; save me,
and I will keep Your instructions.

I rise before dawn and call for help;
I put my hope in Your word.
My eyes are awake before each watch of the night,
that I may ponder Your promise.

In Your faithful love, Yahweh, listen to my voice,
let Your decrees give me life.
The pursuers of corruption draw near;
they are far from Your law.

But You are near, O Yahweh,
and all Your commands are truth.
Long ago I learned from Your instructions
for You have established them for ever.

All: Glory to Abba our God, to Christ the Word,
and to the Holy Spirit.
As it was in the beginning,
is now and will be for ever. Amen.

Antiphon 2

In Your faithful love, Yahweh, listen to my voice,
let Your decrees give me life.

Silent Prayer

READING 1 Peter 4:8-11

(All are seated during the reading.)

Above all, preserve constant love for one another, for love covers over many a sin. Be mutually hospitable without grumbling. Whatever gift each of you may have received, use it in service to one another, like good stewards dispensing the grace of God in its varied forms. Are you a speaker? Speak as one who utters the words of God. Do you render service? Render it by the strength which God grants, in order that in everything God may be glorified through Jesus Christ to Whom glory and dominion belong for ever and ever. Amen.

(After the reading a period of silence may be observed followed by a brief shared reflection.)

RESPONSORY

The judgments of Yahweh are true;
they gladden the heart.
R. The precepts of Yahweh are clear; they give light
to the mind.

Your decrees give me life,
R. they give light to the mind.

Glory to Abba our God, to Christ the Word,
and to the Holy Spirit.
R. The precepts of Yahweh are clear;
they give light to the mind.

GOSPEL CANTICLE

(*All stand for the Canticle of Mary. Incense may be used
during the singing of the Gospel Canticle.*)

Antiphon

I call with all my heart, Yahweh, answer me,
and I will observe Your statutes.

Song of the Virgin Mary - Luke 1:46-55

My soul proclaims the greatness of Yahweh,
my spirit rejoices in God my Savior;
for Yahweh has looked with favor on this lowly servant,
and henceforth all generations will call me blessed:

"You, the Almighty, have done great things for me,
and Holy is Your Name.
Your compassion is from generation to generation
to those who revere You.

You have brought victory with Your strength
and have dispersed the arrogant of mind and heart.
You have pulled down the mighty from their thrones,
and have raised high the lowly.

You have filled the hungry with good things,
and have dismissed the rich empty handed.

You have come to the help of Israel, Your servant,
remembering Your promise of faithful love,
the promise You made to our ancestors,
to Abraham and to his descendants for ever."

All: Glory to Abba our God, to Christ the Word,
and to the Holy Spirit.
As it was in the beginning,
is now and will be for ever. Amen.

Antiphon

I call with all my heart, Yahweh, answer me,
and I will observe Your statutes.

INTERCESSIONS

Jesus said, "The bread I shall give is my flesh for the
life of the world." Let us give thanks to God whose
love nourishes and sustains us everyday of our lives.
With gratitude we pray:
R. Glory to You, Yahweh, our God.

Abba, our God, it is by Your gift that we praise
You—for You wondrously created us and even more
wondrously restored us to grace.
R. Glory to You, Yahweh, our God.

Abba, our God, be with us and with our dear ones—
move our hearts to seek You and our wills to serve
You.
R. Glory to You, Yahweh, our God.

Abba, our God, deepen our awareness of Your presence—teach us to respect and to love all that You
made.
R. Glory to You, Yahweh, our God.

Abba, our God, to know You is to love those You
created—fill our hearts with love for all our brothers
and sisters.
R. Glory to You, Yahweh, our God.

(*Other prayers may be added.*)

THE ABBA PRAYER OF JESUS

CONCLUDING PRAYER

Almighty and ever-living God,
we come reborn in Your Spirit,
and confidently call You Abba our God.
Renew Your Spirit in our hearts
make us ever more perfectly Your children
and bring us to our promised inheritance.
Touch our lives and our hearts,
that we may grow in the love of God,
make us signs of Your love for all people.
We ask this through Christ our Savior.
R. Amen.

BLESSING

May God bless us, protect us from all evil
and bring us to everlasting life.
R. Amen.

GATHERING PRAYERS 20:

You Have Given Me My Heart's Desire.

INTRODUCTORY VERSE

(*All stand and make the sign of the cross as the leader of prayer says*:)

O God, come to my assistance.
R. Yahweh, make haste to help me.

All: Glory to Abba our God, to Christ the Word,
and to the Holy Spirit.
As it was in the beginning,
is now and will be for ever. Amen.

HYMN

(*An appropriate hymn is sung.*)

PSALMODY

(*During the recitation of the psalms all may sit. Two groups may alternate praying the stanzas of the psalm. The antiphon is prayed by the entire group.*)

Psalm 21:1-7,13 A Thanksgiving Prayer

Antiphon 1
You made me glad with the joy of Your presence.
Yahweh, I rejoice in Your power,
and greatly rejoice in Your saving help!
You have given me my heart's desire,
and have not denied the prayer of my lips.

For You have blessed me with blessings of goodness;
and You have set a precious crown on my head.
I asked life of You; You gave it to me,
even length of days for ever and ever.

My glory is great through Your help;
You have bestowed upon me honor and majesty.
You made me most blessed for ever;
You made me glad with the joy of Your presence.

For I trust in Yahweh,
and in the faithful love of the Most High.
Be exalted, O Yahweh, in Your strength!
We will sing and praise Your power.

All: Glory to Abba our God, to Christ the Word,
and to the Holy Spirit.
As it was in the beginning,
is now and will be for ever. Amen.

Antiphon 1
You made me glad with the joy of Your presence.

Silent Prayer

Psalm 119:153-160 God's Law, Our Source of Life: A Meditative Prayer.

Antiphon 2
Your kindnesses to me are countless, Yahweh,
true to Your decrees, give me life.

Look on my affliction and deliver me,
for I do not forget Your law.
Invoke my cause and reclaim me;
give me life according to Your promise!

Salvation is far from the wicked,
for they do not seek Your statutes.
Your kindnesses to me are countless, Yahweh,
true to Your decrees, give me life.

Countless are my oppressors and adversaries,
but I do not deviate from Your instructions.
The sight of these traitors grieves me,
because they do not observe Your promise.

See how I love Your precepts, O Yahweh,
Give me life true to Your faithful love.
The essence of Your word is truth;
and all Your just decrees endure for ever.

All: Glory to Abba our God, to Christ the Word,
and to the Holy Spirit.
As it was in the beginning,
is now and will be for ever. Amen.

Antiphon 2
Your kindnesses to me are countless, Yahweh,
true to Your decrees, give me life.

Silent Prayer

READING 1 Peter 3:8-12

(*All are seated during the reading.*)

All of you should be one in thought and feeling. You should be loving toward one another, tender-hearted and humble-minded. Do not repay one wrong with another, or an angry word with another one; instead, repay with a blessing. That is what you have been called to do, that you may receive a blessing as your inheritance.

Who among you loves life and longs for time to enjoy prosperity? Guard your tongue from evil, your lip from any breath of deceit. Turn away from evil and do good, seek peace and pursue it. For the eyes of Yahweh are turned to the just and Whose ears to their prayer. The face of Yahweh is set against those who do evil.

(After the reading a period of silence may be observed followed by a brief shared reflection.)

RESPONSORY

All of you should be one in thought and feeling.
R. The blessings of God will rest upon you.

What joy to see a family united in love,
R. and the blessings of God will rest upon you.

Glory to Abba our God, to Christ the Word,
and to the Holy Spirit.
R. The blessings of God will rest upon you.

GOSPEL CANTICLE

(All stand for the Canticle of Mary. Incense may be used during the singing of the Gospel Canticle.)

Antiphon

The essence of Your word, O Yahweh, is truth;
and all Your just decrees endure for ever.

Song of the Virgin Mary - Luke 1:46-55

My soul proclaims the greatness of Yahweh,
my spirit rejoices in God my Savior;
for Yahweh has looked with favor on this lowly servant,
and henceforth all generations will call me blessed:

"You, the Almighty, have done great things for me,
and Holy is Your Name.
Your compassion is from generation to generation
to those who revere You.

You have brought victory with Your strength
and have dispersed the arrogant of mind and heart.
You have pulled down the mighty from their thrones,
and have raised high the lowly.

You have filled the hungry with good things,
and have dismissed the rich empty handed.

You have come to the help of Israel, Your servant,
remembering Your promise of faithful love,
the promise You made to our ancestors,
to Abraham and to his descendants for ever."

All: Glory to Abba our God, to Christ the Word,
and to the Holy Spirit.
As it was in the beginning,
is now and will be for ever. Amen.

Antiphon

The essence of Your word, O Yahweh, is truth;
and all Your just decrees endure for ever.

INTERCESSIONS

The eyes of Yahweh, our God, are turned to the meek and humble of heart. Let us pray to God our Creator, Shepherd and constant Helper:
R. Hear us, O God, our Refuge.

We bless You, O God, for You graciously called us to be Your Church—bless us with constant faith and make Your Church a source of life for the world.
R. Hear us, O God, our Refuge.

You have called N., to be the head of the Church—endow him with unfailing faith, living hope and loving concern.
R. Hear us, O God, our Refuge.

Grant us the grace of true conversion—grant to all the grace of repentance and salvation.
R. Hear us, O God, our Refuge.

Christ, Your Incarnate Word, knew what it was to be excluded from one's homeland—be mindful of those who must live far from their family and country.
R. Hear us, O God, our Refuge.

Grant forgiveness to the dead who have put their trust in You—and the peace of eternal rest in heaven.
R. Hear us, O God, our Refuge.

(Other prayers may be added.)

THE ABBA PRAYER OF JESUS

CONCLUDING PRAYER

Almighty and ever-loving God,
the joy You have prepared for those who love You,
is beyond all our imagining.
Your care extends beyond the boundaries of race
and nation to the hearts of all who live.
Fill our hearts with love for all people,
that the walls, which prejudice raises between us,
crumble beneath the shadow of Your outstretched arm.
We ask this through Christ our Savior.
R. Amen.

BLESSING

May God bless us, protect us from all evil
and bring us to everlasting life.
R. Amen.

GATHERING PRAYERS 21:

May My Prayer Be Set Before You Like Incense.

INTRODUCTORY VERSE

(*All stand and make the sign of the cross as the leader of prayer says:*)

O God, come to my assistance.

R. Yahweh, make haste to help me.

All: Glory to Abba our God, to Christ the Word,
and to the Holy Spirit.
As it was in the beginning,
is now and will be for ever. Amen.

HYMN

(*An appropriate hymn is sung.*)

PSALMODY

(*During the recitation of the psalms all may sit. Two groups may alternate praying the stanzas of the psalm. The antiphon is prayed by the entire group.*)

Psalm 141:1-5 Prayer for Protection from Wickedness

Antiphon 1

May my prayer be set before You like incense,
my uplifted hands like an evening sacrifice!

I call to You, Yahweh, hasten to me,
listen to my voice when I call to You!
May my prayer be set before You like incense,
my uplifted hands like an evening sacrifice!

Set, O Yahweh, a guard over my mouth,
guard, O Most High, the door of my lips!

Incline not my heart to an evil word,
to perform vicious deeds with the wicked;
in company with evildoers,
let me not partake of their dainties!

Let the just chastise and rebuke me,
it shall be a kindness;
let not the wicked anoint my head with oil,
for my prayer has been against their wickedness.

All: Glory to Abba our God, to Christ the Word,
and to the Holy Spirit.
As it was in the beginning,
is now and will be for ever. Amen.

Antiphon 1

May my prayer be set before You like incense,
my uplifted hands like an evening sacrifice!

Silent Prayer

Psalm 119:161-168 God's Law, Our Source of Joy and Hope: A Meditative Prayer.

Antiphon 2

Seven times a day I praise You, O Yahweh,
for all Your decrees are just.

Rulers persecute me without cause,
because my heart delights in Your word.
I rejoice at Your promise
as one who finds great fortune.

I detest and disdain deceit,
but I cherish Your law.
Seven times a day I praise You
for Your just decrees.

Great peace is to those who love Your law;
nothing can make them stumble.
I wait for Your salvation, O Yahweh,
and I follow Your commands.

My soul observes Your instructions;
and I love them very much.
I observe Your precepts and instructions,
for all my ways are known to You.

All: Glory to Abba our God, to Christ the Word,
and to the Holy Spirit.
As it was in the beginning,
is now and will be for ever. Amen.

Antiphon 2

Seven times a day I praise You, O Yahweh,
for all Your decrees are just.

Silent Prayer

READING 2 Peter 1:19-21

(*All are seated during the reading.*)

So we are even more confident of the message proclaimed by the prophets. You will do well to be attentive to it, because it is like a lamp shining in a dark place, until day dawns and the light of the morning star shines in your hearts. Above all else, remember this, no prophecy of scripture is a matter of one's interpretation, because no prophecy ever came by human will, but rather human beings moved by the Holy Spirit spoke under the influence of God.

(After the reading a period of silence may be observed followed by a brief shared reflection.)

RESPONSORY

I will sing for ever of Your mercy O Yahweh.
R. I will make known to all generations Your mercy.

I wait for Your salvation, O Yahweh,
R. and make known to all generations Your mercy.

Glory to Abba our God, to Christ the Word, and to the Holy Spirit.
R. I will make known to all generations Your mercy.

GOSPEL CANTICLE

(All stand for the Canticle of Mary. Incense may be used during the singing of the Gospel Canticle.)

Antiphon

I observe Your precepts and instructions,
for all my ways are known to You, O Yahweh.

Song of the Virgin Mary - Luke 1:46-55

My soul proclaims the greatness of Yahweh,
my spirit rejoices in God my Savior;
for Yahweh has looked with favor on this lowly servant,
and henceforth all generations will call me blessed:

"You, the Almighty, have done great things for me,
and Holy is Your Name.
Your compassion is from generation to generation
to those who revere You.

You have brought victory with Your strength
and have dispersed the arrogant of mind and heart.
You have pulled down the mighty from their thrones,
and have raised high the lowly.

You have filled the hungry with good things,
and have dismissed the rich empty handed.

You have come to the help of Israel, Your servant,
remembering Your promise of faithful love,
the promise You made to our ancestors,
to Abraham and to his descendants for ever."

All: Glory to Abba our God, to Christ the Word,
and to the Holy Spirit.
As it was in the beginning,
is now and will be for ever. Amen.

Antiphon

I observe Your precepts and instructions,
for all my ways are known to You, O Yahweh.

INTERCESSIONS

Jesus says: Those who eat my flesh and drink my blood will live for ever; I shall raise them to life on the last day. We pray that we be united with God and all of God's people as we pray:
R. Unite us in Your love.

You have called us to be heralds of the Good News—help us to enter the depths of the gospel message and to make it our own.
R. Unite us in Your love.

Teach us to build a more humane world—teach us to respect the dignity of all our brothers and sisters.
R. Unite us in Your love.

Protect and defend those who are discriminated because of race, color, sex, class, language or religion beliefs—let their dignity be respected and their rights upheld.
R. Unite us in Your love.

Welcome all who have died in Your peace—bring them to everlasting life with all Your holy ones.
R. Unite us in Your love.

(Other prayers may be added)

THE ABBA PRAYER OF JESUS

CONCLUDING PRAYER

Almighty God,
all truth is from You,
and Your grace makes us one in mind and heart.
Give Your people the joy
of hearing Your word in every sound
and of longing for what You promise.
May all the attractions of a changing world
serve only to bring us the peace of Your reign.
We ask this through Christ our Savior.
R. Amen.

BLESSING

May God bless us, protect us from all evil
and bring us to everlasting life.
R. Amen.

GATHERING PRAYERS 22:
O God, You Are Compassionate.

INTRODUCTORY VERSE

(All stand and make the sign of the cross as the leader of prayer says:)

O God, come to my assistance.
R. Yahweh, make haste to help me.

All: Glory to Abba our God, to Christ the Word,
and to the Holy Spirit.
As it was in the beginning,
is now and will be for ever. Amen.

HYMN

(An appropriate hymn is sung.)

PSALMODY

(During the recitation of the psalms all may sit. Two groups may alternate praying the stanzas of the psalm. The antiphon is prayed by the entire group.)

Psalm 116:1-9 Hymn of Thanksgiving

Antiphon 1

O Yahweh, You are gracious and just;
O God, You are compassionate.

I love Yahweh
Who listens to the sound of my prayer,
Who bends down to listen to me,
Whom I will implore all my life.

The traps of death encircled me;
the agony of Sheol came upon me;
I was overcome by distress and anguish.

Then I called on the Name of Yahweh:
"Deliver me, Yahweh, I beseech You.
O Yahweh, You are gracious and just;
O God, You are compassionate.

O Yahweh, You look after the simple;
when I was powerless, You gave me strength."
"Return, O my soul, to your rest;
for Yahweh has treated you kindly"

"For You have rescued my soul from death,
my eyes from tears, my feet from stumbling;
that I may walk before You, Yahweh,
in the land of the living."

All: Glory to Abba our God, to Christ the Word,
and to the Holy Spirit.
As it was in the beginning,
is now and will be for ever. Amen.

Antiphon 1

O Yahweh, You are gracious and just;
O God, You are compassionate.

Silent Prayer

Psalm 119:169-176 God's Law, A Meditative Prayer.

Antiphon 2

May my lips proclaim Your praise
for You have taught me Your statutes.

May my cry come into Your presence, Yahweh;
give me wisdom according to Your word!
May my prayer come into Your presence;
rescue me according to Your promise!

May my lips proclaim Your praise
for You have taught me Your statutes.
May my tongue recite Your promise,
for all Your commands are just.

May Your hand be ready to help me,
for I have chosen Your precepts.
I long for Your salvation, Yahweh,
Your law is my delight.

May I live only to praise You,
may Your decrees be my help.
If I should go astray like a lost sheep,
come and look for Your servant,
for I have not forgotten Your commands.

All: Glory to Abba our God, to Christ the Word,
and to the Holy Spirit.
As it was in the beginning,
is now and will be for ever. Amen.

Antiphon 2

May my lips proclaim Your praise
for You have taught me Your statutes.

Silent Prayer

READING Philippians 2:2-4,14-15

(All are seated during the reading.)

Make my joy complete by being of a single spirit, one in love, one in heart and one in mind. Do nothing out of jealousy or vanity, instead, in humility regard others as better than yourselves. Let each of you pursue not your own interests, but those of others.

Do all you have to do without murmuring or questioning. Remain blameless and pure, as God's perfect children surrounded by corrupt and godless people. You must shine among them like stars lighting up the sky.

(After the reading a period of silence may be observed followed by a brief shared reflection.)

RESPONSORY

Remember Your tender mercies, O Yahweh.
R. I long for Your mercy for Your law is my delight.

May my prayer come into Your presence;
R. for Your law is my delight.

Glory to Abba our God, to Christ the Word,
and to the Holy Spirit.
R. I long for Your mercy for Your law is my delight.

GOSPEL CANTICLE

(All stand for the Canticle of Mary. Incense may be used during the singing of the Gospel Canticle.)

Antiphon

May my cry come into Your presence, Yahweh;
give me wisdom according to Your word!

Song of the Virgin Mary - Luke 1:46-55

My soul proclaims the greatness of Yahweh,
my spirit rejoices in God my Savior;
for Yahweh has looked with favor on this lowly servant,
and henceforth all generations will call me blessed:

"You, the Almighty, have done great things for me,
and Holy is Your Name.
Your compassion is from generation to generation
to those who revere You.

You have brought victory with Your strength
and have dispersed the arrogant of mind and heart.
You have pulled down the mighty from their thrones,
and have raised high the lowly.

You have filled the hungry with good things,
and have dismissed the rich empty handed.

You have come to the help of Israel, Your servant,
remembering Your promise of faithful love,
the promise You made to our ancestors,
to Abraham and to his descendants for ever."

All: Glory to Abba our God, to Christ the Word,
and to the Holy Spirit.
As it was in the beginning,
is now and will be for ever. Amen.

Antiphon

May my cry come into Your presence, Yahweh;
give me wisdom according to Your word!

INTERCESSIONS

God calls us to shine in the world like stars lighting up the sky. Let us offer our praise and prayers to God who knows all that we need:
R. We praise You, O God.

We bless You, Yahweh God, the Creator of the universe—though we are sinners, You have called us to the knowledge of Your truth.
R. We praise You, O God.

Yahweh God, You opened the gates of mercy for us—let us never turn aside from the path of life.
R. We praise You, O God.

We celebrate the new life You give us in Christ our Savior—help us to spend this day in the spirit joy and peace.
R. We praise You, O God.

Grant us Your faithful people a prayerful spirit of gratitude—that in all things may we offer You praise and thanksgiving.
R. We praise You, O God.

(Other prayers may be added.)

THE ABBA PRAYER OF JESUS

CONCLUDING PRAYER

Almighty and all-forgiving God,
every good and perfect gift comes from You.
Infuse in our hearts a desire to please You
and fill our minds with insight into love,
so that every though may grow in wisdom
and all our efforts may be filled with Your peace.
Increase our zeal for Your service,
and bring to perfection the gifts given us.
We ask this through Christ our Savior.
R. Amen.

BLESSING

May God bless us, protect us from all evil
and bring us to everlasting life.
R. Amen.

LIGHT SERVICE

(After the Introductory Verse the leader of prayer lights an oil lamp or a candle as may be convenient. During the lamp/candle lighting one of the following prayers is said or an appropriate hymn sung or silence kept. Incense may be used during the light service as a sign of the community's prayer rising to God.)

1. Christ Our Light.
> Jesus Christ is the Light of the World.
> a light no darkness can extinguish.

2. Light my Light.
> Light my Light, the world-filling Light,
> the eye-kissing Light, heart-sweetening Light!
> The Light dances at the center of my life,
> the Light strikes the chords of my love.
> > Tagore

3. Lead Me
> Lead me from untruth unto truth,
> Lead me from darkness unto light,
> Lead me from death unto life.
> Shanti (Peace) Shanti, Shanti.
> > Katha Upanishads

4. You Are Light.
> You who are Light, brighten me with your light.
> You who are Power, fill me with power.
> You who are Courage, infuse courage into me.
> You who are Strength, give me strength.
> You who are Vital Essence, endow me with vitality.
> You who are Fortitude, fill me with fortitude.
> > Yajur Veda

5. Enlighten Our Hearts, O God!
> Let us be united;
> Let us speak in harmony;
> Let our minds apprehend alike.
>
> Common be our prayer;
> Common be the end of our assembly;
> Common be our resolutions;
> Common be our deliberations.
>
> Alike be our feelings
> Unified be our hearts,
> Common be our intentions;
> Perfect be our unity.
> > Rig Veda

6. Om . . . Shanti - Shanti - Shanti
> May God protect us,
> May God guide us,
> May God give us strength,
> May God give us right understanding.
> May love and harmony be with us all.
> May there be Shanti (Peace).
> > Upanishads

7. God Be In My Head
> God be in my head, and in my understanding;
> God be in my eyes, and in my looking;
> God be in my mouth, and in my speaking;
> God be in my heart, and in my thinking;
> God be in my end, and in my departing.
> > Sarum Primer

8. You Are Everything to Me
> You are my Father,
> You are my Mother.
> You are my Kith and Kin,
> You are my Friend.
>
> You are my Learning,
> Only You are my Wealth.
> You are the God of Gods,
> You are Everything to me.
>
> Oh my Loving Father and Mother,
> Lead me from untruth unto truth,
> Lead me from darkness unto light,
> Lead me from death unto life.
> > Katha Upanishads

9. God Is Shanti (Peace).
> May there me peace in the higher regions;
> may there be peace in the firmament;
> may there be peace on earth.
> Shanti (Peace) - Shanti - Shanti
>
> May the waters flow peacefully;
> may the herbs and plants grow peacefully;
> may all the divine powers bring unto us peace.
> Shanti (Peace) - Shanti - Shanti
>
> May we be all in peace,
> peace and only peace;
> and may that peace come unto each of us.
> Shanti (Peace) - Shanti - Shanti!
> > Rig Veda

OPTIONAL CANTICLES

1. The Song of Zechariah - Luke 1:68-79

"Blessed are You Yahweh, the God of Israel,
You have come to Your people and set them free.
You have raised up for us a mighty Savior,
born of the house of Your servant David.

You promised through the mouth
of Your holy prophets from of old,
that You would save us from our enemies,
from the hands of all who hate us.

You promised to show mercy to our ancestors,
and to remember Your holy covenant.

This was the oath You swore to our ancestor Abraham:
to set us free from the hands of our enemies,
that we may be free to serve You without fear,
and be holy and just in Your sight all our days."

"And you, my little child,
will be called the prophet of the Most High;
for you will go ahead of the Savior
to prepare a straight path,
and to give the people knowledge of salvation
through the forgiveness of their sins.

In the tender compassion of our God,
the Dayspring from on high will visit us
to shine on those who dwell
in darkness and in the shadow dark as death,
and to guide our feet into the way of peace."

2. Song of the Lamb - See Revelation 19:1-7

Salvation and glory and power to our God,
Whose judgments are true and just.
R. Alleluia, alleluia!

"Praise our God, all you God's servants,
all who revere God, small and great."
R. Alleluia, alleluia!

Yahweh our God the Almighty reigns.
Let us rejoice and let us sing praise.
R. Alleluia, alleluia!

Let us give glory to our God,
for the wedding feast of the Lamb has begun.
R. Alleluia, alleluia!

3. The Song of Simeon - Luke 2: 29-32

Yahweh God,
now You let Your servant go in peace;
Your Word has been fulfilled.

For my eyes have seen Your salvation
which You have prepared for all peoples:
a light to reveal You to the nations
and the glory of Your people, Israel.

4. A Song to God the Creator - Revelation 4:11,5:9-10,12

"Worthy are You, O Yahweh our God,
to receive glory and honor and power.

For You created all things,
and by Your will they continue to exist."

"Worthy are You, O Lamb of God,
to receive the scroll
and to break open its seals.

For You were sacrificed
and by Your blood you ransomed people for God
of every race, language, people and nation.

You made them to be a royal race
and priests to serve our God,
and they shall reign on earth."

"Worthy is the Lamb that was sacrificed,
to receive power, riches, wisdom
strength, honor, glory and blessing!"

5. Song of the Redeemed - Revelation 15:3-4

Great and glorious are Your works,
O Yahweh God the Almighty!

Just and true are Your ways,
O Sovereign Ruler of the nations!

Who shall not revere and glorify Your Name?
For You alone, O Yahweh, are holy.

All nations shall come and worship You,
for Your judgments have been revealed."

6. Song of the Easter Mystery - Philippians 2:6-11

Jesus, being in the form of God,
did not consider equality with God
something to be grasped.

But, Jesus emptied one's self,
taking the form of a slave,
being born in human likeness.

And being in every way like a human being,
Jesus was humbler yet,
even to accepting death, death on a cross.

And for this God has highly exalted Christ,
and designated the name Jesus
which is above all other names;

So that all beings,
in the heavens, on earth and under the earth,
should bend the knee at the name of Jesus;

And every tongue should proclaim
that Jesus Christ is Kyrios (Lord),
to the glory of Abba our God.

7. Let Us Give Thanks to Abba God - Colossians 1:12-20

Let us give thanks to Abba God,
for making us worthy to share
in the inheritance of the saints in light.

God has delivered us from the dominion of darkness
and assigned us to the Realm of Christ, the Beloved,
in whom we have redemption, the forgiveness of
sins.

Christ is the image of the invisible God,
the first-born of all creation;
for in whom all things were created,
in heaven and on earth, things visible and invisible.

All things were created through Christ,
all things were created for Christ,
who is before all things,
and in whom everything continue in being.

Christ is the Head of the Body, the church;
the One who is the Beginning,
the First-born from the dead,
the One who is preeminent in everything.

It pleased God to make absolute fullness reside in
Christ
in whom and through whom to reconcile all things
both on earth and in heaven,
making peace by the death on the cross.

8. Song of Thanks for Salvation - Ephesians 1:3-10

Blessed be the God
and Abba of our Savior Jesus Christ,
who has bestowed on us in Christ,
every spiritual blessing in the heavens.

God chose us in Christ
before the foundation of the world,
to be holy and blameless,
and to be full of love.

God predestined us to be children
through Jesus Christ,
in accord with the divine will and pleasure,
that all might praise the glorious grace
which was freely bestowed on us in the Beloved.

In Christ we have redemption through the blood,
the forgiveness of our wrongdoings,
for so immeasurably generous is God's favor
that is lavished upon us.

God has given us wisdom and insight
to understand fully the mystery,
according to the divine plan
which was carried out in Christ.

A plan to be carried out
in the fullness of time:
to unite all things in Christ,
things in heaven and things on earth.

9. A Song of Praise - Daniel 3:52-57

Blessed are You, Adonai, God of our ancestors;
highly exalted and glorified for ever.
Blessed is Your holy and glorious Name;
highly to be praised, exalted above all for ever.

Blessed are You, glorious in Your holy temple;
most worthy to be glorified above all for ever.
On the throne of Your majesty between the Cherubim:
highly exalted, glorified above all for ever.

Blessed are You, who behold the depths,
worthy of praise, highly exalted for ever.
Blessed are You in the firmament of heaven;
worthy to be glorified in hymns for ever.

Let the whole creation give glory to Abba our God,
to Christ the Word, and to Rooha the Spirit.
Most worthy to be glorified in hymns of praise,
now and always and for ever and ever. Amen

10. Canticle - 2 Timothy 2:11-13

If we have died with Christ,
we shall also live with Christ;

If we persevere,
we shall also reign with Christ.
But if we deny Christ,
then Christ also will deny us.

Even if we are unfaithful,
Christ remains faithful—
for Christ cannot deny one's own self.

11. Canticle on Love - 1 Corinthians 13:4-13

Love is always patient and kind;
love is never jealous;
love is not boastful or arrogant.

Love is never rude or selfish;
Love is not irritable or resentful;
Love does not rejoice at wrongdoing,
but finds its delight in truth.

Love is always ready to bear all things
to believe all thing and to hope all things
and to endure whatever comes.

Love never comes to an end;
as for prophecies, they will pass away;
as for tongues, they will cease;
as for knowledge, it will pass away.

For our knowledge is imperfect
and our prophecy is imperfect;
but when the perfect comes,
the imperfect will pass away.

When I was a child, I used to speak like a child,
think like a child, reason like a child;
when I became an adult, I put aside childish ways.

At present we see indistinctly, as in a mirror
but then face to face.
At present I know in part;
then I shall understand fully,
even as I am fully known.

As it is these three remain
faith, hope, and love,
but the greatest of them is love.

12. Canticle in Praise of Creation - Daniel 3:56-88

Let the whole creation bless Yahweh:
Give praise and glory to Yahweh for ever.
In the mighty firmament of heaven, bless Yahweh:
Give praise and glory to Yahweh for ever.

All you angels and powers of God, bless Yahweh:
You heavens and waters above, bless Yahweh:
You Sun and moon and stars of heaven, bless
Yahweh:
Give praise and glory to Yahweh for ever.

Shower and dew, and winds that blow, bless Yahweh:
Fire and heat, Cold and warmth, bless Yahweh:
Sleet and falling snow, bless Yahweh:
Give praise and glory to Yahweh for ever.

Frost and chill, ice and snow, bless Yahweh:
Nights and days, light and darkness, bless Yahweh:

Lightening and clouds, bless Yahweh:
Give praise and glory to Yahweh for ever.

Let the earth bless Yahweh:
Mountains and hills, bless Yahweh:
Everything growing from the earth, bless Yahweh:
Give praise and glory to Yahweh for ever.

You flowing springs, seas and rivers, bless Yahweh:
You whales and all water creatures, bless Yahweh:
All you birds of the air, bless Yahweh:
Give praise and glory to Yahweh for ever.

You beasts of the wild, bless Yahweh:
All you flocks and herds, bless Yahweh:
O men and women everywhere, bless Yahweh:
Give praise and glory to Yahweh for ever.

Let Israel, people of God, bless Yahweh:
You priests of God, bless Yahweh:
You servants of God, bless Yahweh:
Give praise and glory to Yahweh for ever.

Spirits and souls of the just, bless Yahweh:
You faithful and humble in heart, bless Yahweh:
Hananiah, Azariah, and Mishael, bless Yahweh:
Give praise and glory to Yahweh for ever.

Give praise and glory to Abba our God,
to Christ the Word, and Rooha the Spirit.
In the mighty firmament of heaven,
Give praise and glory in hymns for ever.